green guide

DANGEROUS CREATURES
....
OF AUSTRALIA

Martyn Robinson
Series Editor: Louise Egerton

NEW
HOLLAND

First published in 2002 by
New Holland Publishers (Australia) Pty Ltd
Sydney • London • Cape Town • Auckland

1/66 Gibbes Street Chatswood 2067 Australia
Garfield House 86 Edgware Road London W2 2EA United Kingdom
80 McKenzie Street Cape Town 8001 South Africa
218 Lake Road Northcote Auckland New Zealand

Reprinted in 2003 (twice), 2005, 2006, 2007 (twice), 2008

Important Note: First aid is vital but books can only give general guidelines. Medical assistance
should always be sought where diagnosis or medical attention is required. Neither author nor
publishers can take any responsibility for any results, effects or outcomes connected with any
advice of method provided in this book, however caused.

Series Editor: Louise Egerton
Project Editor: Fiona Doig
Design: Nanette Backhouse
Picture Research: Kirsti Wright
Production Controller: Wendy Hunt
Reproduction by: Pica Digital, Singapore
Printed and bound by: Kyodo Nation Printing Services

National Library of Australia Cataloguing-in-Publication Data:

    Robinson, Martyn.
    Dangerous creatures of Australia.

    Includes index.

    ISBN(13) 978-1-86436-663-1
    ISBN(10) 1 86436 663 X.

    1. Dangerous animals — Australia. I. Egerton, Louise. II.
    Title. (Series : Green guide (New Holland)).

    591.650994
The body copy is set in 9pt Cheltenham Light.

Photographic Acknowledgments
Abbreviations NHIL = New Holland Image Library; LT = Lochman Transparencies
Photograph positions: t = top; b = bottom; c = centre; m = main; i = inset; l = left; r = right; fc = front
cover; bc = back cover; m = main. **Shaen Adey/NHIL**: p. 65t; **Kelvin Aitken**: bcb, p. 4b, 5t, 56–57, 65b, 66t,
67t, 67b, 90b; **Kathie Atkinson**: fcl, fcb, bct, p. 3, 7t, 7b, 14t, 14b, 15b, 19m, 29t, 30t, 37i, 38t, 38b, 41m, 41i,
42i, 43i, 47, 51t, 52m, 52i, 55b, 58b, 63m, 77i, 78t, 82t, 83b, 84b, 87b, 88t, 88b, 89b, 90t, 91b; **Bill Belson/LT**:
p. 13t; **Hans & Judy Beste/LT**: p. 13b, 18m, 18i, 25i, 35m, 60m, 60i; **Eva Boogaard/LT**: p. 62m, 68b, 74b;
Robert Brunet: p. 48b; **Clay Bryce/LT**: fci, p. 4t, 9t, 61i, 71t, 80m, 81m, 81i, 83t, 87t; **Neville Coleman**: p.
58t, 61m, 64t, 69c, 69b, 72t, 72b, 73t, 75t, 75b, 78b, 79t, 85tr, 85tl, 92t, 92b, 93b; **James Cook University/Dr
Jamie Seymour**: p. 91t; **John Cooper**: p. 19i; **G. A. Eldon**: p. 63i; **Pavel German**: p. 5r, 6b, 27i, 30b, 31b,
32t, 36–37, 48t, 57i; **Ken Griffiths**: fcm, p. 5lb, 12t, 16b, 17b, 20t, 20b, 24m, 24i, 27m, 29b, 33t, 34i, 53m, 62i;
Karen Gowlett-Holmes: p. 68t, 82b, 85b; **Dr C. Andrew Henley**: p. 17t; **Rudie Kuiter**: p. 69t; **Jiri
Lochman/LT**: p. 10–11, 11i, 12b, 20c, 26m, 39b, 40m, 40i, 42m, 44t, 54b; **Peter Marsack/LT**: p. 53i; **Leo
Meier/NHIL**: p. 59b; **Dr Stuart Miller/LT**: p. 23b; **NHIL**: p. 59t; **Peter & Margy Nicholas/LT**: p. 70t,
70b, 79b, 84t, 86b; **Col Roberts/LT**: p. 73b; **Dennis Sarson/LT**: p. 15t, 21t, 55t; **Jay Sarson/LT**: p. 16t;
Gunther Schmida/LT: p. 8t; **Raoul Slater/LT**: p. 6t; **Alex Steffe/LT**: p. 71b; **St John Ambulance
Australia**: p. 9b; **Geoff Taylor/LT**: p. 21b; **Twilight Zone Photographics/Rebecca Saunders**: p. 66b,
74t, 76–77, 86t; **Western Australian Museum**: p. 93t; **Dept. of Medical Entomology, Westmead
Hospital**: p. 45b; **Steve Wilson**: p. 22t, 22b, 23t, 25m, 26i, 28t, 28b, 31t, 32b, 33b, 34m, 35i, 43m, 44b, 46i,
51b, 54t, 80i; **Paul Zborowski**: p. 8b, 39t, 45t, 46m, 49t, 49b, 50t, 50b, 64b, 89t.

CONTENTS

Introduction to Dangerous Creatures

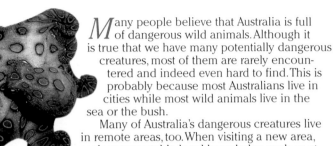

*M*any people believe that Australia is full of dangerous wild animals. Although it is true that we have many potentially dangerous creatures, most of them are rarely encountered and indeed even hard to find. This is probably because most Australians live in cities while most wild animals live in the sea or the bush.

Many of Australia's dangerous creatures live in remote areas, too. When visiting a new area, seek out reputable local knowledge, such as at the nearest national parks office. Locals are familiar with the day-to-day problems they encounter and know best how to avoid them. Tourist information centres are also good places to enquire about dangerous wildlife.

Beautiful but deadly — a blue-ringed octopus.

Pretty Spectacular

Some of Australia's dangerous creatures are impressive in more ways than one. The blue-ringed octopuses, for example, are not only the world's deadliest octopuses, they are also the most colourful. Australia's bull ants may be formidable stingers but they are also the world's largest worker ants. The thought of an

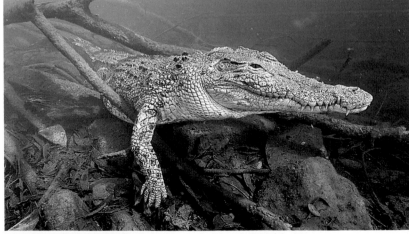

The impressive Saltwater Crocodile; its kind has survived from the time of the dinosaurs.

enormous crocodile or shark cruising by us may send shivers down the spine but such magnificent creatures rarely fail to impress us. In fact, sharks are not the threat urban legends would have us believe. Very few species are known to attack humans.

Snakes and Spiders

We have quite a few venomous snakes and several dangerous spiders. Most snakes keep to themselves and they are uncommon in cities. Attacks most often happen when the snake is either trodden upon or when it is being harassed. Spiders are better able to cope with urban life and the most deadly spider of all is a common inhabitant of some Sydney suburbs, yet even with this species, bites are rare.

Bradley's Mouse Spider, like the similar-looking funnel-webs, may be dangerous.

The Death Adder is uncommon in cities.

Keeping Safe

Most wild animals are not interested in hurting human beings. The best way to keep safe is to leave wild animals alone. Don't offer them food or try to touch them. Don't try to kill them either unless absolutely necessary as it is when they are threatened that many serious attacks occur.

This book will help you to identify and learn a little about those Australian animals that sometimes pose a threat to us. Armed with this knowledge you are less likely to find yourself in dangerous situations.

POISON VS VENOM: KNOW THE DIFFERENCE

'Poisonous' and 'venomous' does not mean the same thing. Venomous animals can introduce venom into your bloodstream by biting, stabbing, stinging or spiking. Poisonous animals, on the other hand, must be eaten. There are, for example, several Australian fish that are poisonous but not venomous. They will make you ill only if you eat them. Other fish may have spines, barbs or even a bite that, on penetration of the skin, release venom into your system.

Does Australia Have Many Dangerous Animals?

*A*ustralia has some of the most diverse, unique and potentially dangerous wildlife in the world. We have more venomous snakes than any other country, both the world's most venomous spiders and the world's most venomous octopuses. Living in our oceans are venomous stonefish, many large sharks and several marine stingers, including the deadly Box Jellyfish; and in our tropical estuaries lurks the

Australia has two species of crocodiles. The biggest, shown here, is the human-eating Saltwater Crocodile.

gigantic Saltwater Crocodile. We even have dangerous ants and, most surprising of all, a venomous — but nonetheless delightful — mammal, the Platypus.

Why Do Animals Attack Us?

*I*n most cases animals attack humans in self-defence. Very few set out to harm us but accidents can happen. If, for example, you accidentally step on a snake or if a spider gets trapped in your clothing, you may be bitten. When the animal cannot get away, it panics and bites the perceived threat. In other cases, it is a case of mistaken identity. For example, if while you are swimming you brush against a jellyfish or are bitten by a shark, the animal probably mistook you for a more manageable meal.

Another reason why animals sometimes attack is in order to defend their young. If you happen to get too close to a broody cassowary or magpie, for example, the bird may attack you in defence of its nest or young.

Yet a third reason for attacks arises from humans behaving with unwarranted

A snake under attack is always fiercer than one sunning itself quietly or going about its business.

aggression towards animals. This can happen when we react too quickly and out of fear. For example, a snake will often bite someone who tries to kill it when it had no intention of biting them in the first place. So always try to remain calm when faced with a frightening animal — it may be quite harmless. Most Australians very rarely encounter a serious problem with the wildlife. A bite from a mosquito, sandfly or some other annoying bloodsucking parasite is about as serious as it gets for the majority of people.

Why Protect Dangerous Animals?

*P*art of the reason wildlife attacks are so rare is because the animals themselves are rare and becoming more so every day. Sadly, humans cause their deaths, both directly and by destruction of their habitat, far more frequently than they cause ours.

Many of the world's most magnificent creatures, such as lions and elephants, are dangerous, but few people question the wisdom of protecting them. Indeed, tourists travel huge distances and spend a great deal of money just to see such animals in their natural habitat. This is true of Australian animals, too. People love to see crocodiles lounging around on the banks of rivers in the Top End, some even delight in coming face to face with a Great White Shark from the relative safety of an underwater shark-proof cage.

A funnel-web spider being milked for its venom.

> ### AN INSECTICIDE WITH VENOM
> In laboratory trials the venom of funnel-web spiders has proved an invaluable ingredient in insecticides. Many spiders depend upon insects for their food. So, it is perhaps little wonder that the venoms they have developed are specifically targeted for insects.

Creators of Wealth and Health

Dangerous animals make other contributions, too. The lucrative crocodile-farming industry brings employment and wealth to northern Australia. We also harvest delicious honey from honeybees. Spiders are great pest controllers and their silk is used in microsurgery. Leeches, too, are used in medicine — to help maintain blood flow while severed appendages, such as fingers or ears, are reattached.

Life-giving Venom

The toxic venoms of many Australian creatures are proving useful in medicine. Taipan venom, for example, helps in the manufacture of fibrin film, a membrane used for wrapping nerves or tendons, and covering organs such as the brain during surgery. It can be left in the body to dissolve harmlessly, avoiding the need for further surgery. Eastern Brown Snake venom has been used in identifying abnormalities in blood clotting. Red-back Spider venom is showing promise in the treatment of high blood pressure and stroke. Ongoing research into Australian animal venoms is likely to have further useful medical applications.

Mulga or King Brown Snakes are milked to produce antivenom.

Are Injuries from Animals Common?

Although this copperhead is dangerous, it is shy and, like most snakes, prefers a quiet life.

*N*o. Injuries inflicted by Australian animals are quite rare. Serious injury or death is extremely rare. Stories of deaths caused by animals receive a lot of media coverage precisely because they *are* rare, and the stories are often wildly exaggerated.

Wild Claims

People will sometimes tell you scary stories about what certain animals did which are completely untrue. For example, funnel-web and Red-back spiders cannot jump and snakes very rarely chase people. In fact snakes have low levels of exertion and a limited field of vision. In most cases they do not even know what they are moving towards. As far as they are concerned you are as likely to be a tree as a human being.

The truth is that humans are more at risk of injury by a motor vehicle than by any animal. The most deadly monsters in this world move on four wheels or two legs, not eight, six, four or no legs at all. The table below gives statistics for humans that have been killed in the ten years between 1980 and 1990. Note how few incidents are caused by animals.

Red-back Spiders may be dangerous, but they do not jump.

ACCIDENTAL CAUSE OF DEATH 1980–1990			
Road Accidents	32 772	Bee Sting	20
Suicide	18 836	Snake Bite	18
Drowning	3 367	Marine Animals*	12
Murder	3 106	Shark Attack	11
Poison	1 998	Crocodile Attack	8
Struck by Lightning	19	Spider Bite	1

*other than sea snakes, crocodiles and sharks

Source: Australian Bureau of Statistics, Australian Natural History 1992–93, vol. 24, No 23, pp 46–53

What Sort of Injuries Do Animals Inflict?

*I*njuries vary from superficial scratches and bruises through to life-threatening venomous bites. For treatment of serious injuries, see pages 94–95. Treatments vary according to the type of injury.

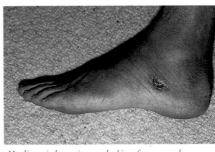

Healing nicely: a tiger snake bite after one week.

- **Envenomation.** When venom penetrates skin and enters the bloodstream.
- **Poisoning.** From eating poisonous flesh, such as that of toadfish.
- **Bruising, punctures and lacerations.**
- **Infection.** Such as Ross River fever, malaria or following an injury, like septicemia from a crocodile bite.
- **Electrocution.** Yes, a few unusual Australian fish, such as torpedo rays and numbfish, can give a nasty electric shock if handled or stepped on.
- **Rashes.** From hairs or spines left embedded in the skin.

What Precautions Can You Take ?

*M*ost of Australia's dangerous animals only attack when they feel threatened. If you take a few sensible precautions, you can enjoy the bush without worrying about the wildlife.

First-aid kits come in a variety of sizes and are available from chemists, and disposal and camping stores.

Some Handy Hints

- Keep your distance from potentially dangerous animals. Do not try to interfere with them or harm them in any way.
- In areas where snakes may live, such as long grass or boggy places, wear thick boots, long socks and long trousers. Watch carefully where you are treading. It is also a good idea to stomp as you move. Snakes are sensitive to vibration and may slide away if they sense you coming.
- Where there are mosquitoes, wear insect repellent.
- Where there are ticks, try not to touch vegetation. Lavender oil has a good reputation as a tick repellent.
- Bushwalkers should carry a first-aid kit. If you bushwalk a lot or work in the bush, do a first-aid course so you know exactly what to do in an emergency.
- If a potentially dangerous animal enters your home or yard, call an animal-rescue service (see page 97 for emergency numbers).

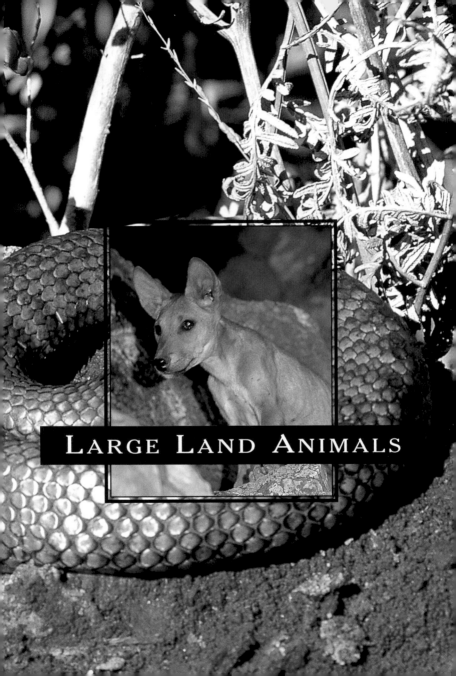

LARGE LAND ANIMALS

Which Large Land Animals Are Dangerous?

Small children can be easily knocked over by over-enthusiastic Pelicans.

*Y*our first thought would probably be snakes but snakes are not commonly encountered and many of them are quite harmless. You might be surprised to hear that there are several mammals and birds that also sometimes cause injuries. Several wild or feral animals that are generally not regarded as dangerous should also be approached with care.

When Domestics Go Wild

In Australia domesticated camels, horses, donkeys and water buffalo have all, at one time or another, been released or escaped into the bush. Just because these animals are descended from domestic stock does not mean they are tame and docile now. Indeed these animals can kick painfully hard if cornered. Except for the water buffalo — which bears potentially lethal horns — they can bite, too. Brumby stallions and bull camels will often attack riders on geldings or females of their own species travelling through their territories.

A kick from a camel you can live without.

Pigs have also escaped and been released into the bush and wild pigs can grow alarmingly stout tusks.

Among our native mammals, the large kangaroos have been known to kick humans with their powerful hind legs, causing considerable injury. Again, only when the animal feels threatened is it likely to react aggressively.

This said, most city people will never encounter these wild animals. They are creatures of the outback and bush.

Snatch and Duck

Among our feathered friends, cassowaries, emus and ostriches can deliver a powerful kick capable of causing fractures or worse. These birds may be provoked into action by human encroachment, so keep your distance. They may be defending nests or young. The notorious Australian Magpie has

SELLING CAMELS TO EGYPT

Yes, it's true. Australia is exporting its feral camels to Egypt. They are apparently remarkably fit and healthy, and not prone to some of the many diseases that plague the domesticated Egyptian stock.

a spring-time tendency to dive-bomb hapless walkers who venture near its nest. Broody swans and geese, too, will bite or strike out with their strong wings. Even owls have on occasion attacked people attempting to climb their nest trees.

Some birds take advantage of human handouts. Emus have been known to snatch sandwiches from startled picnickers. Pelicans may pester fishermen and even knock over small children with their wings in their rush to get fed. Feeding wild animals is never recommended.

What Is the Golden Rule About Wildlife?

*L*eave wild animals alone. Unless you are familiar with a particular animal, it is best to treat it with caution. Accidental injuries can occur even when an animal is friendly. Many large animals cause damage inadvertently or when acting in self-defence. For example if someone tries to catch a goanna they find wandering around, the animal is quite likely to bite, scratch and lash out with its tail in an attempt to be left alone.

Australia's largest goanna, the Perentie, nonchalantly swings by to check out the picnickers food supply.

Injuries also result from people trying to feed wild animals. This brings animals in close contact with humans and some wild animals come to expect a free feed. For example, never hand-feed goannas. They are not very good at distinguishing between the food and a proffered hand, so you may just get bitten. Severe bites often become infected because goannas regularly feed on carrion.

A Case of Mistaken Identity

Goannas sometimes make visual mistakes. A frightened goanna dashing to the nearest vertical object to climb out of harm's way, may inadvertently climb up the leg of a horse or human rather than a tree or fencepost. People have suffered minor lacerations from the animal's sharp claws, not to speak of the terrible shock.

Wildlife sanctuaries only expose their gentlest animals to the public.

Feral Pigs

Feral Pigs can grow up to 1.5 m in length and reach a weight of 115 kg. They are descended from domestic pigs that either escaped or were released. When dogs are present, or when they are cornered, wounded, hungry or guarding their young, feral pigs can be quite dangerous. On a few occasions they have even been known to enter rural suburbs in groups to raid garbage bins and urban gardens. If disturbed, they usually run away but do not rely on it. Their main weapons are their sharp

Where there's one Feral Pig, there's usually more.

tusks, which are borne by both males and females. If a pig seems aggressive, back away to the nearest tree and be prepared to climb it. Rock outcrops are also good as long as they are steep enough to defeat a pig's poor climbing abilities.

Feral Pigs prefer wet areas with access to watercourses for wallowing, but they are very adaptable and may be found in all kinds of habitat, from the arid inland to the mountains and the coast.

They live in all States, except Tasmania, and are even known from some off-shore islands. Under favourable conditions, they may produce up to ten young in a litter and perhaps two litters a year.

Water Buffalo

Water Buffalo reach 1.8 m in length, weigh up to 1180 kg and bear an impressive set of horns. They roam the grassy floodplains of the Top End where they churn up the swamps and river banks with their cloven hooves and graze on grasses and other vegetation.

Domesticated animals are docile and most wild buffalo will run away from intruders but sometimes a buffalo behaves unpredictably

Water Buffalo may seem docile but these large animals can be unpredictable and may charge.

ASIAN IMPORT
The Water Buffalo was imported because it is well-adapted to the tropics. Domesticated for centuries in Asia, it was thought the ideal beast of burden for the hotter, wetter parts of this country.

and becomes aggressive, especially if it is wounded or harassed. Never tease a buffalo. It may charge, even at a vehicle. In such an event — if on foot — seek out the nearest climbable tree quickly!

The Water Buffalo is nowadays mainly restricted to Arnhem Land and adjacent areas in the Northern Territory. Some animals, however, have wandered all the way into Western Australia and Queensland.

Never offer food to a Dingo.

Dingoes

Dingoes have had an uneasy relationship with humans in recent times. Found in all States except Tasmania, they were probably brought over from Southeastern Asia by Aboriginal Australians thousands of years ago. Some Dingoes are completely wild. Others have lost their wariness of humans and serious problems have arisen.

Tame or semi-tame Dingoes, such as those on Fraser Island or near Uluru, are actually more dangerous than wild ones. They may hang around campsites hoping to be fed, raid unattended supplies and refuse to go away. These problems have arisen mostly from people feeding them or bothering them. In some cases, Dingoes have been known to bite, so always keep your distance and never attempt to pat or pick up a wild Dingo or its pup. Reputedly more dangerous to domestic stock than pure Dingoes are Dingo–domestic dog crosses.

Kangaroos

Male Eastern Grey Kangaroos sparring. Leaning back on their tails leaves their powerful legs free for kicking.

Some large kangaroos grow to 1.9 m nose-to-tail, weigh 66 kg and can be quite intimidating. Species such as Red Kangaroos, Eastern and Western Grey Kangaroos and Euros are not normally dangerous, despite their size, but they are capable of causing harm if they feel cornered.

As a rule wild kangaroos flee at the approach of humans. Semi-tame animals, however, present a greater risk. They may treat a human as they would another kangaroo, grappling with their forepaws, leaning well back on their tails to provide enough support to lift and kick with both hind legs simultaneously. Such a blow could break a man's ribs while the long claws are quite capable of ripping flesh.

Kangaroos in zoos and parks where people can enter enclosures are usually not a threat as troublesome animals are generally removed but it is a good idea to keep a watch on young children. If you are concerned about entering such an area, ask someone in charge if it is safe to pat the kangaroos. Avoid any kangaroo that coughs or rears up very tall as though it is stretching — these are both signs of aggression,

When Do Some Birds Get Mean?

This Black Swan will vigorously protect its young cygnet.

*T*here are two particular occasions when some birds are known to become especially mean. The first is when they are nesting or protecting their young. The second is when they have become accustomed to being fed by humans and start to get pushy.

The swans in your local park, for example, may become transformed during the breeding season from a picture of grace and serenity into a flurry of charging feathers with wings and neck outstretched; it may hiss furiously. Swans and geese can bite and a blow from a swan's wing can cause a fracture.

Is It Safe to Handle Injured or Sick Birds?

*I*njured birds sometimes misinterpret a rescue attempt by wildlife carers as a threat. They may lash out to 'defend' themselves, causing injuries such as deep lacerations, pecks and bites. Be careful with any species you are not familiar with as many have a surprisingly long reach with their beaks or claws.

Also, some bird diseases can affect people. For example, psittacosis is transmitted by inhaling a disease-causing organism from sick birds or even from the dust of their cages. Carers should wear masks when dealing with suspect birds or while cleaning out their cages, and wash their hands immediately after contact. In addition use gloves, cloths, towels or something similar to pick up injured birds. Members of the heron and bittern family should always be handled with care. One hand should always keep hold of the beak, otherwise the frightened bird might peck powerfully at the face or eyes.

This Sulphur-crested Cockatoo is being syringe-fed by a wildlife carer.

Why Do Magpies Attack?

*P*robably the most common bird attacks come from Australian Magpies. Every spring, while they are nesting, these maggies develop unpredictable and aggressive behaviour towards perceived invaders. They undertake aerial attacks upon passers-by, often children on their way to school. Swooping from behind and clacking their beaks, their attacks can be startling, especially to those with a heart condition. Cyclists under attack may swerve and have an accident. Just occasionally a rogue magpie pecks someone deeply enough to draw blood and every year several people end up in hospital. Magpies seem to pick on certain types of people. It may be people with red hair, postal workers or a schoolchild. Recent studies show that when both sexes of magpies attack, it is a case of birds regarding people as nest predators. In attacks by male magpies only, however, it seems more a matter of proving to his mate what a good nest defender he is.

DUCK FOR PLOVER

Nesting Spur Winged Plovers, or Masked Lapwings, sometimes launch aerial attacks on people in parks. If someone unwittingly ventures too close to their well-camouflaged eggs on the ground, they may swoop, squawking loudly, and strike with their sharp wing spurs, potentially drawing blood.

A bicycle helmet affords good protection in the magpie season.

Defending Yourself

The easiest defence is to take another route until the nesting season is over. Alternatively, try holding a leafy branch above your head, as magpies aim for the tallest part of their victim. Small children can protect themselves by wearing an ice-cream container as a helmet. This can be particularly effective if you draw false eyes, or even glue sunglasses, onto the back of the hat.

Aerial raids by nesting magpies have resulted in some curious headware among small schoolchildren.

Southern Cassowary

An adult male cassowary accompanies his chick on a foraging mission. Inset: One hard kick from a foot like this can be serious, or even fatal.

The Southern Cassowary is one of three flightless birds living in Australia. Adults tower 2 m tall and may weigh a hefty 58 kg. They are normally shy and, until recently, were rarely seen. Their natural habitat is the dense rainforest and overgrown tropical swamps of Far North Queensland but as the cassowary's rainforest home has been cleared for housing and agriculture, these stately birds have inevitably had closer contact with humans. Some locals and tourists hand-feed them and this has resulted in some undesirable effects. In the wild they eat fallen fruit, fungi, insects and other small animals but when food is scarce they may venture into urban areas, orchards and picnic grounds. They have even been known to eat road-kills. Birds may snatch food from unwary hands and can become aggressive, so do not feed them and give them a wide berth and a clear escape route.

Role Reversals

Southern Cassowaries breed when rainforest fruits are plentiful, usually June to October. The female typically lays four eggs but it is the male that incubates them and raises the chicks. In their desire to protect their young, nesting birds and those with chicks can be aggressive and they are armed with long claws.

> **PLANTING SEEDS**
> Cassowaries swallow rainforest fruits whole, digesting the flesh rapidly and passing out the seeds undamaged. This helps spread new plants to new areas. So these birds contribute a great deal to the health and growth of rainforests.

Australian Magpie

The Australian Magpie can be aggressive during the spring breeding season. Inset: A demanding brood keeps maggie parents on the go.

Despite the reputation of Australian Magpies for aerial bombardments during the nesting season, they are generally quite placid and mind their own business. They are common throughout most of Australia except for Far North Queensland, the Northern Territory and parts of central West Australia, and are often seen in urban and rural areas. Although their native habitat is open eucalypt woodlands, where they forage for worms, insects, lizards, small vertebrates, berries and seeds, they find playing fields and lawns rich picking grounds.

Magpies often venture quite close to humans and they are easily tamed. Indeed they have been known to just walk into houses through open doors. Do not be afraid. A little patience and guidance back out of the door is all that is required.

They have a delightfully mellifluous song and can mimic other sounds, including human speech. They are very different in temperament and habits from the somewhat similar-looking currawongs which have a distinctly yellow eye.

Parenting Strategies

Magpies only breed when they can find and defend a nesting territory. In bushland areas, they often nest assisted by a clan of helpers. Usually older siblings will help raise, feed and protect the chicks of a strong pair. In urban areas where food is plentiful, single pairs may raise young without help. Immature birds often roam the bush in large nomadic flocks.

Should You Be Scared of Snakes?

*N*o. Of Australia's seven snake families, four pose virtually no threat to humans. The pythons, for example, may be big but they have no fangs. The worm-like blind snakes are completely harmless, small, smooth earth-burrowers and the file snakes that inhabit the billabongs of Australia's tropical north are also harmless. The fourth group, the colubrids have a few venomous species but their fangs — through which the venom is channelled — are generally small and set far back in their mouths.

The real threat to humans comes from the land-based elapids. Members of this group inject venom through fangs set at the front of their mouths. Not all have powerful enough venom to seriously harm humans. In fact, only 25 or so species of snakes out of 384 known species in Australia are regarded as potentially deadly. In addition about 22 species of the 32 sea snakes around the coast should be considered dangerous but there has not been a single verified death from sea-snake bite ever recorded in Australia.

Do not mess with this snake. It is an Eastern Brown, possibly the most common deadly snake in Australia.

Pythons have no fangs and make surprisingly good pets.

Can You Identify a Snake by Its Colour?

This juvenile Eastern Brown Snake looks nothing like the adult above.

*R*arely. Skin colour varies greatly, even in a single species. To start with there are regional differences. Also skin colour often changes with age. Most importantly, snakes are always sloughing off their old skin. Underneath their new skin is usually much brighter and more colourful.

There are one or two Australian snakes that change their colour to regulate their body temperature. The Inland Taipan is perhaps the best example of this. As its name suggests, this snake lives in the inland areas of Australia, where summer temperatures are baking hot during the day but winter night-time temperatures are surprisingly low. To accommodate these seasonal fluctuations, the Inland Taipan has evolved the ability to change skin colour to both reflect and absorb the heat.

Unfortunately — both for the snakes and the humans — identifying snakes is quite difficult. Enquire at your State museum or local park authority about what snakes are common in the area. Then use a field guide to identify those. Gradually you will learn to tell the difference.

What Can You Do for a Snake Bite?

*D*on't panic and don't try to kill the snake. Your first attention should go to the victim.

Immobilise the wounded limb as indicated on page 94. Keep the patient calm and seek medical help as soon as possible. Whenever you can, get the patient to hospital. Here, tests can be run to determine

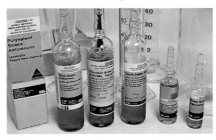

Antivenom used for snakebite treatment is specific to each type of snake venom, so identification is important.

which species has bitten the patient and medical staff can administer the appropriate antivenom.

There are antivenoms for most species and most people recover fully from even the most potent bites. Only a very few have a reaction to the antivenoms.

MILKING SNAKES

There are people who 'milk' snakes all the time. These skilful operators collect venom not milk — from venomous snakes. The venom is then used to make an antivenom. When the antivenom is injected into some-one who has been bitten by a venomous snake its effect should fully counter the effect of the bite. Australian antivenoms are regarded as the world's safest.

How Fast Can a Snake Move?

*A*lthough snakes strike quickly and give the impression of great speed, most of them cannot go any faster than a brisk walk, so you can easily outrun a snake.

Probably the world's fastest snake is Africa's Black Mamba, which can slither at a disarming 18 km/h for brief bursts. Australia's fastest may be the Black Whip Snake, which readily outpaces the small lizards it feeds upon, some of which are surprisingly fleet of foot.

Most snakes cannot move faster than a brisk walking pace.

Which Snake Has the Most Toxic Venom?

*T*he Inland Taipan has the most toxic venom of any land snake in the world and it can also deliver a lot of venom in a single bite due to its robust venom glands. Despite this, it should not be considered a great threat. As far as we know, it has never been known to kill anyone. Its distribution is very remote and it has a retiring and shy disposition. The very few people known to have been bitten by one have all survived after treatment. However, these were mainly professional reptile collectors who knew proper snake bite first-aid and would have had help available close by. A knowledge of first-aid procedure is invaluable.

As far as we know, the Inland Taipan has caused no deaths.

Which Is Australia's Deadliest Snake?

*W*hile its venom is a little less potent than the Inland Taipan, the Common Taipan usually injects a larger quantity. Because it lives in areas where humans are relatively common, it is considered Australia's deadliest, although not its most toxic, snake. As far as snake-bite figures show, the brown snake group has killed the most people since records began in 1979. Tiger snakes were the next in the number of fatalities, followed by Common Taipans and death adders.

It is worth bearing in mind that these statistics may be more a reflection of where most people live rather than the lethal nature of particular snake species.

THE LEAST LETHAL SNAKE

Estimating which one of Australia's venomous snakes is the least lethal is a difficult question. This is because many of our snakes that have venom strong enough to kill people have never been recorded as doing so and this includes the Inland Taipan.

The Common Taipan is regarded as Australia's deadliest snake.

Do All Snakes Have Fangs?

*N*o. In Australia none of the pythons, worm snakes or file snakes have fangs. Neither do most of the colubrid snakes but some have small fangs positioned at the rear of their mouths. To humans, these snakes are harmless.

In Australia for a snake to be considered dangerous to a human its fangs must be positioned at the front of its mouth and the venom must be powerful enough to affect us. Sea snakes, as well as snakes of the elapid family — which contains

The Brown Tree Snake, a rear-fanged colubrid, gapes widely to increase its chances of fangs contacting prey.

all of our deadly land snakes — have fangs at the front of their mouths. If the fangs are long enough, they can pierce human skin and inject venom into our bloodstreams. This is why we fear them. Fangs are hollow or grooved teeth; most snakes have teeth but only venomous snakes have fangs.

Which Australian Snake Changes Colour?

*T*he Inland Taipan changes colour according to the season. During summer it is light coloured for camouflage and to reflect excess heat. During winter it often turns darker to absorb heat so it has the energy to move and to digest food. At other times a black-headed phase allows it to warm itself while exposing only its head. This means that they can emerge and hunt earlier, while it's still cool and so avoid the heat of the day.

Unlike many lizards, colour-change in snakes is unusual. Only the Inland Taipan and the rare Oenpelli Python are known to have this ability. A few, like the Green Tree Snake, may seem to change colour by puffing itself up to reveal coloured skin between each scale but this colour was always present — only hidden.

An Indian Cobra showing its hood.

FAMILY (NECK)TIES

Many Australian venomous snakes are related to the Asian cobras. The link becomes apparent when black and tiger snakes flatten their necks 'cobra-fashion'. The expanded neck makes the snake look larger and so more threatening. When this posturing is accompanied by loud hissing, many potential predators are persuaded to back off and pursue less threatening prey.

Brown Snakes

Of all Australian snakes, the browns have killed the most people. Above: A Western Brown Snake or Gwardar. Inset: An Eastern Brown Snake.

Brown snake is a name commonly given to seven different species. Although the upper bodies of these snakes are usually brown, grey or reddish, their bellies may be spotted, banded, cream, yellow, orange or grey. It is safest to treat any slender snake that fits the above description with caution.

Although venomous, the Speckled and Ringed Brown Snakes pose no serious threat as they are only 50 cm long when full-grown. The other five species grow to 1 m or more and are therefore considered potentially dangerous.

The Dangerous Five

Occurring throughout mainland Australia, brown snake species live everywhere except rainforests. Species are best determined by region and habitat. The Dugite (1.5 m) of southwestern Western Australia inhabits dunes, heaths and desert shrublands, while the nearly-identical Peninsula Brown Snake (1.2 m) is mainly restricted to the Eyre Peninsula, South Australia. Ingram's Brown Snake (1.2 m) lives on the Barkly Tablelands of Queensland and the Northern Territory, often within the cracks of drying grasslands.

The Western Brown Snake or Gwardar (1.5 m) is absent only from the extreme east and southern Australia to southwestern western Australia. It is widespread throughout drier parts of Australia and tropical grasslands. The Eastern Brown Snake (1.5 m), on the other hand, is a common visitor to farmlands along the eastern and southern coast, and further inland (see map). It also frequents the outer suburbs of Sydney and Adelaide.

Taipans

The Inland Taipan's venom is the world's most toxic snake venom but the Common Taipan (inset) is more frequently encountered.

Taipans are extremely dangerous snakes and should be treated with utmost care. The good news is that they are not very commonly encountered. The two Australian species carry large quantities of highly toxic venom and their strike is fast and deadly. Their victims are usually bandicoots, rodents and lizards. They have absolutely no interest in humans but, if a taipan is wounded or cornered, there is always the possibility of a strike.

The Inland Taipan is rarely seen as it inhabits the remote floodplains where Queensland, New South Wales, South Australia and the Northern Territory meet, and there are a few records from near the Victoria–New South Wales border. A long snake (2.5 m), brownish yellow, sometimes with vague dark bands, its head is often distinctly black. Its preferred prey is the Long-haired Rat, which it chases down into mud cracks and burrows.

The Common Taipan

The Common Taipan is slightly smaller than its inland relative (2 m) but it is still a large snake. It inhabits a wide range of habitats from northeastern New South Wales up into Cape York in Queensland and across the northwest of the Northern Territory into northeastern West Australia. It is still feared in sugarcane-growing areas, where it sometimes enters the fields in search of rats.

SUGAR AND SNAKES
Before the coming of sugarcane harvesters, sugarcane was cut by hand. One of the risks of cane-cutting then was being bitten by Common Taipans who had ventured into the canefields in pursuit of prey, namely the several species of rats that proliferated there.

Tiger Snakes

An Eastern Tiger Snake's stripes are usually distinct (above), unlike those of a Black Tiger Snake (inset).

Tiger snake bites are very potent and quite a large amount of venom may be injected in a single bite. They can easily kill an adult human and are responsible for an average of one death a year. The venom works by attacking the nervous system and the muscles, and by clotting the blood.

Tiger snakes can be grey to brown above and usually have paler bands, sometimes yellow; hence their name. There are three species. The most widespread and commonly encountered is the Eastern Tiger Snake, which occurs in the mountainous areas of southeastern Queensland and northern New South Wales, on both sides of the Great Dividing Range, across Victoria and into southeastern South Australia. It is absent from the northeastern New South Wales coast. The Black Tiger Snake, which confusingly has no 'tiger' stripes but is black all over, is found in Tasmania and on islands of the Bass Strait, and the Western Tiger Snake inhabits southwestern Western Australia.

Where to Beware

Tiger snakes generally prefer watercourses and swampy areas. They look for food in the grasses and reeds and can climb low shrubs. They are mainly frog-eaters but will take small reptiles, mammals and birds, and have even been known to eat stranded fish. Paddling with bare feet in the grassy or reedy swamps of tiger-snake country, especially where frogs are breeding, is not advised. Also take care after dark as these snakes often wander about on warm nights.

FECUND TIGERS
All tiger snakes produce live young and the Eastern Tiger Snake must hold the record with a maximum of 109. The young resemble adults in their colour pattern.

Death Adders

Deadly and camouflaged, the Common Death Adder (above) and Desert Death Adder (inset) wait for prey.

There is no mistaking a death adder once you see it, but seeing it isn't always easy. These snakes are relatively short and fat and have a wedge-shaped head. The banding of grey, red or brown on the body is distinctive, as is the way it suddenly peters out to a narrow tail tipped with a contrasting colour — usually cream.

Unfortunately death adders are not always seen as they blend well with their surroundings and they often sun themselves on bush paths, partially hidden beneath leaf litter where unwary humans may step on them. Usually sluggish, they strike with lightning speed. Bushwalkers should wear thick socks and sturdy shoes and carry a torch to light their way at night around the campsite.

WHAT'S IN A NAME?
Despite their appearance and name Australian death adders are more closely related to the cobras than they are to European or African adders. Interestingly in some areas they are known as 'deaf' adders, which is quite accurate. All snakes are deaf and lack external ear openings.

Distribution of the Three Species

Three species are recognised. The Desert Death Adder inhabits Australia's arid centre. The Northern Death Adder lives across northern Australia from the Kimberley to Cape York. The Common Death Adder is found in eastern Queensland, New South Wales and the southern edge of South Australia and Western Australia but it is absent from Tasmania, Victoria, the southern edge of New South Wales and Cape York in Queensland.

How Can I Avoid Attracting Snakes?

Snakes are often attracted to houses and buildings, especially in rural areas. There are many reasons for this but most often they are attracted there by food, such as mice, rats or frogs living around or under buildings. If you wish to deter snakes, there are a number of simple measures you can take.

Remove piles of timber, corrugated iron or rocks from near the house. Stack the timber and iron upright and some distance away. Upright stacks are far less appealing snake homes than those lying flat on the ground. Keep grass and lawns as short as possible around the house and build frog ponds and chicken coops a good distance from the main buildings.

Rodents, chooks and frogs attract snakes.

Why Do Some Snakes Produce Live Young?

Egg-laying has many advantages. The mother has to spend less time carrying around the extra weight; little or no care is required once the eggs are laid, and several clutches can be laid over the breeding season. However, the degree of control that the mother has over the development of her offspring is limited. Also, if the weather is cold, the eggs will take much longer to develop and the embryos might even die. Predators can easily find eggs and eat them.

> **BLACK IS WHITE**
> There have been several albino Red-bellied Black Snakes found over the years, which must be one of the few situations when black really is white. All black snakes have potentially dangerous bites.

In some reptiles, the sex of the young is determined by the temperature at which the eggs are incubated. If it is too hot or too cold, the parent ends up with offspring that are all the same sex. As a result, many reptiles — particularly those from cold areas — retain their eggs internally until they are ready to hatch as live young.

This means that in cold weather, the mother can bask in the sun to raise both her own temperature and that of her developing young. She can also escape from predators when warmed. If she belongs to one of the sex-determined-by-temperature species, she can even-out the sex ratio of her young by varying her own temperature. Tiger snakes, death adders and copperheads all fall into the live-birth category.

These young Dugites from Western Australia have hatched from eggs laid by their mother.

Are New Snake Species Evolving?

Several of the islands in Bass Strait have populations of Black Tiger Snakes. On some islands the Black Tiger Snakes eat muttonbird chicks almost exclusively. These are only available for a short time each year during the nesting season. The chicks grow rapidly and soon they become too big for the snakes to swallow, so the snakes must gorge themselves while the chicks are still small. For the rest of the year, they starve as there is little or no other food for them on the island.

Sitting duck... well actually a muttonbird chick, a standard on the menu of some island Black Tiger Snakes.

Because availability and type of prey differs from island to island, as do conditions, tiger snakes have had to adapt. As a result, the snakes found on one island are often quite different in appearance from those on another, even though they may live only a short distance apart. Eventually they can become so different from their neighbours that even if they could cross breed, they may no longer produce viable offspring. They are then said to be different species.

What Is the Tale of the Adder's Tail?

Animals that use a part of their body, or certain actions, to entice prey species are said to be using aggressive mimicry. Death adders are one of the few reptiles to use this hunting technique — they wriggle their tails in front of their mouths to lure their prey. Small lizards, birds and the like, attracted by this worm-like lure to come closer, are then caught by the snake.

Shortly after their birth, a whole litter of baby adders may start wiggling their tails at the sight of a small lizard or other potential food.

Although death adders are fast to strike at their prey, occasionally they are not fast enough — several death adders have been found minus their white tail tips.

Come and get it. Is it a worm? No, it's a tail.

Red-bellied Black Snake

Red-bellied Black Snake: common in many areas.

The Red-bellied Black Snake is common in many areas, even close to suburbs. To many people it is the most familiar dangerous snake in Australia. It is shiny black above and red or pinkish below, with a length of 1.5–2.1 m. It can be found along eastern Australia from southeastern South Australia to northern Queensland, usually in swampy areas. It is mainly a frog-eater, but also takes small mammals and reptiles.

The Red-bellied Black Snake is a shy animal. Given the opportunity it will slip away quietly, so do not panic if you see one. This snake is usually reluctant to bite — even under provocation — and bites that do occur often need little or no medical treatment. Nevertheless, do not rely on this being the case. If someone is bitten, you should seek medical help to be on the safe side.

Collett's Snake

Just how venomous Collett's Snake really is has yet to be assessed but its relatives have a fiercesome reputation.

Probably one of Australia's most colourful reptiles, Collett's Snake is 1.5 m long, brown to black above with irregular blotches, and bands of cream to pink scales. Although potentially deadly, it is rarely encountered as it lives in remote areas of central Queensland, often in black-soil country. In this landscape, the soil is often dry for large parts of the year and it forms cracks where Collett's Snake shelters from the scorching sun and looks for food. When the soil cracks close up, after the wet season, the snake becomes more visible and active, hunting for small mammals, like rodents, and reptiles such as small lizards. This species has been successfully bred in captivity and recorded as laying approximately 12 eggs in a clutch. Unfortunately, because of its restricted distribution and scarcity, very little more is known about it.

Mulga Snakes

Mulga Snakes should be regarded as potentially dangerous as they are known to have caused deaths. Up to 2 m long, their body colouring ranges from light brown to red–brown to almost black. Each scale has a dark end and a lighter front end resulting in a patterned appearance.

Two-tone scales give the Mulga Snake its patterning.

Often a thick-set species, the Mulga is also referred to as a King Brown Snake. This is probably due to its large size, colouring, and its diet, which sometimes includes other venomous snakes, although frogs, mammals and other reptiles are also included. It lives in the forests of the tropics, in the arid inland and almost everywhere else-except the southeastern coast and ranges, Victoria, Tasmania and the southern edge of the continent. This snake will only harm you if you step on it, pick it up or try to kill it.

Butler's Snake, or the Spotted Mulga Snake, is a potentially dangerous Western Australian relative that inhabits the mulga scrub of the southwest's centre. Dark brown to black with pale patches, it is not known to have caused any fatalities.

Spotted or Blue-bellied Black Snake

While the Spotted or Blue-bellied Black Snake has not been known to cause any deaths, it should never-theless be considered potentially dangerous. Its venom is extremely toxic but it delivers only a small quantity in a single bite.

This snake grows to 1.5–2 m long and, as its common names suggest, it is quite variable in colouration. Some-times it is all black, sometimes black with light scattered spots or even cream with black flecking. Its belly may be blue–grey. From southeast-ern Queensland

A Spotted or Blue-bellied Black Snake laying eggs.

to northeastern New South Wales, it inhabits floodplains, forests and inland areas, where it feeds on small mammals, other reptiles and frogs. It is a shy snake that prefers to remain hidden. If provoked, however, it is liable to flatten itself out and hiss loudly at its tormentor.

The Eastern Small-eyed Snake is usually quite small but it has caused at least one human death.

WHY SMALL EYES?

An efficient tongue is more use to this snake than good vision. Hunting at night, it uses its tongue to 'sniff out' little lizards and snakes that hide under logs, leaf litter and rocks.

Eastern Small-eyed Snake

The Eastern Small-eyed Snake normally measures around 50 cm long but exceptional specimens reach up to more than 1 m. Like all four species described on these two pages, it can certainly inflict a painful bite. Its venom is said to be myotoxic, which means that it attacks the muscles. So far only one human death has been recorded from this muscle damage.

This rather shiny black snake has either a pink or cream belly and is sometimes mistaken for a small Red-bellied Black Snake. It is found all along the east coast of Australia, including the Great Dividing Range, but is absent from Tasmania. It is primarily a lizard-eater and hunts among rocks, logs and leaf litter for its prey. It gives birth to live young but is not a prolific breeder, producing no more than eight young in a batch.

Rarely seen, even by wildlife experts, the chances of being bitten by this snake are extremely few.

Pale-headed Snake

Although not known to have caused any human deaths, the Pale-headed Snake is potentially dangerous. It is 60 cm long, grey to brown, usually with a pale neck-band and a pale grey head. An irregular black blotch behind the pale band on its neck distinguishes it from other species.

This nocturnal snake is found in eastern Australia from just north of Sydney to Cape York in Queensland. It inhabits wooded areas, from rainforests to dry woodlands, and often climbs trees. It shelters in hollows and, from beneath loose bark, ambushes frogs and lizards.

Even experienced reptile collectors do not commonly see this snake and, as a result, the National Parks and Wildlife Service has listed it as vulnerable. This apparent scarcity may in part be due to its ability to remain well hidden.

The Broad-headed Snake will become aggressive when it is threatened.

Broad-headed Snake

The Broad-headed Snake is black with yellow dots and narrow bands. It is 60 cm long and is sometimes confused with a small Diamond Python. Unlike the harmless python, this species can be very aggressive when threatened and has quite potent venom. People have been bitten when, mistaking it for a python, they have tried to pick it up. Bites have also occurred as a result of removing bush-rock, the disturbed snake acting in self-defence.

Broad-headed Snakes are restricted mainly to Hawkesbury sandstone and other rocky outcrops in the Sydney Basin. Occasionally they are found in the hollows of trees. They mainly eat lizards and especially geckoes.

These snakes are now rare because land clearing and bush-rock collection has robbed them of their habitat. They are listed as endangered and studies are currently underway to determine their numbers, the locations of populations and how best to protect them.

Stephens Banded Snake

The Stephens Banded Snake can vary quite dramatically in its markings.

Stephens Banded Snake is a dark brown snake with pale or yellow–brown bands. Some specimens are only blotched or even completely unbanded, making them difficult to identify. While usually about 60 cm long, it can grow to almost 1 m.

Living mostly in wet forests from Gosford in New South Wales to south-eastern Queensland, Stephens Banded Snake is an good climber, both of rocky outcrops and trees. It largely eats lizards, small birds and mammals.

Like its relatives, this snake reacts aggressively when provoked and may bite repeatedly. The venom is quite toxic and the bite should regarded as potentially dangerous. Fortunately it is nocturnal and so rarely seen, although it has been reported crossing roads passing through rainforest at night, particularly during warm weather.

Copperheads

The Lowland Copperhead (above) has less barred lips than are apparent on the Highland Copperhead (inset).

Copperheads are potentially dangerous snakes with a southerly distribution. They normally inhabit swampy areas and are well adapted to the cold, often being the last snakes to disappear before winter and the first to emerge in spring. Usually shy, they may strike if provoked. Their venom attacks the nervous system and the bloodstream and, although no deaths have been recorded, it is potent enough to kill a human.

Copperheads are variable in colour. Above they may be black through to copper-coloured; below may be cream, yellow or red–orange. The lips are usually pale and the head dark. When conditions are good and food, such as frogs and lizards, is abundant, large copperhead populations can build up.

Lowland, Highland and Pygmy Copperheads

The are three species of copperhead. The Lowland Copperhead (1.4 m) lives along the southeastern edge of South Australia and New South Wales, in southern Victoria and northeastern Tasmania as well as on the Bass Strait Islands. The darkest of the three, the Pygmy or Dwarf Copperhead (60 cm), is found only on Kangaroo Island and in the Mount Lofty Ranges of South Australia. Its conservation status is considered vulnerable. Generally considered to be the most colourful member of this group, the Highland Copperhead (1.3 m) is found in the highlands of New South Wales and in eastern Victoria.

> **CHILLY SNACKS**
> Copperheads mainly eat frogs and lizards. By being active at cooler temperatures they can prey upon other cold-blooded animals that have become sluggish, such as reptiles. There is also less competition for food as many snakes are already hibernating. Copperheads hunt night and day if necessary.

Other Venomous Snakes

Two snakes to beware of: the Clarence River Tiger or Rough Scaled Snake (above) and the slender Lesser Black Whip Snake (inset).

Clarence River Tiger Snake

The Clarence River Tiger Snake, or Rough Scaled Snake, (1 m) is not a true tiger snake, although the link is not all that misplaced as it usually has a banded colour pattern on a brownish or olive-coloured body. Often, though, the dark bands are indistinct or incomplete. It even has similar venom, producing similar symptoms which respond to the same antivenom. Several people have died from this snake's bite, so beware. Hunting mostly in daytime in rainforests and wet areas, it has an unusual distribution, with one population south of Cairns and another straddling the Queensland–New South Wales border around the Clarence River, with none recorded in between.

Whip Snakes

All whip snakes are shy and bites are rare, but the Great Black Whip Snake, which can grow to 1.5 m, has made some people seriously ill, although fatalities have not been recorded. This snake ranges in colour from light brown to blackish, often with a paler head patterned with dark flecks. So far it is known only from Cape York in northern Queensland, the far north-west of the Northern Territory and far northeastern Western Australia. Almost identical is the Lesser Black Whip Snake, which is also considered dangerous. Its range is similar except that it extends further down the east coast of Queensland. The only obvious differences are in its slightly shorter length and lack of dark spots on the head. Other whip snakes are not a serious threat to humans. They are all daytime hunters of lizards that rely on speed, not stealth, to catch prey. The Greater Black Whip Snake, for example, has been seen catching rapidly fleeing lizards.

SMALL LAND ANIMALS

Which Small Land Animals are Dangerous?

You might think that being small precludes being dangerous but Australia is well-known for its deadly spiders, and there are a host of other small animals in the bush that unwittingly make life unpleasant for us humans. In rainforests, leeches suck our blood, in swamps sandflies and mosquitoes pump us with skin irritants. There are stinging caterpillars on plants, stinging scorpions beneath rocks and blood-sucking ticks that can cause paralysis. Even the infamous cane toad can harm us if we should accidentally touch its poisonous gland and wipe our eyes or mouth afterwards.

The abdomen and stinger of a bull ant.

The Hymenoptera Mob — a Bunch of Stingers

Ants, bees and wasps all belong to the insect group Hymenoptera (meaning 'membrane wing') and many species bear a stinger attached to a venom gland. Most of these insects can sting repeatedly — only the introduced European Honeybee is a once-only stinger. It has a barbed sting that tears free of its body as it jabs it into a victim — effectively disembowelling it.

While the venom from these creatures is painful, it is rarely lethal. To prevent the venom gland from pumping venom further into the wound, remove the sting quickly and carefully. Do not squeeze it or more venom will be injected. Scratch it out sideways with a long fingernail or knife blade, or lift it out with fine forceps, grasping the sting below the venom gland.

The sting of a European Honeybee embedded in skin.

Allergic Reactions

Serious effects occur for most people only with massive amounts of venom from many stings. However a surprising number of people are allergic to the stings of bees, wasps and ants, and especially European Honeybees. With each sting, reactions often increase in severity until even one can prove fatal. The compounds responsible for the reaction are called histamines. To counteract them, allergy-prone people should take antihistamines.

How Can I Avoid Being Stung?

*M*ost ants, wasps and bees attack only if their lives or nests are directly threatened, so the best way to avoid being bitten is to avoid them whenever you can.

Bull ants are notorious for delivering painful stings to human trespassers.

Children are naturally curious but they should be discouraged from investigating the nests of ants, bees and wasps.

> **DUAL PURPOSE STINGERS**
> Only female bees, wasps and ants sting. Except for the European Honeybee's barb, their stingers are actually modified egg-laying tubes, called ovipositors.

Accidents Do Happen
Sometimes getting stung is unavoidable. Usually this elicits no more than a yelp of pain and maybe an hour or less of discomfort. There are a few precautions, however, you can instigate.

Stinging insects may stumble into clothes on the washing line, so position your line away from vegetation. Spiders may crawl into letterboxes or shoes left outside, especially during rain. Always check them carefully before thrusting a hand or foot inside. One of the worst accidents occurs when a bee or wasp crawls into a can of drink and, unaware, someone takes a swig. A nasty sting to the throat can be fatal for anyone, so medical help should be sought immediately.

A Cure for Ant Stings
Bull ants are large ants capable of injecting sizable amounts of quite potent venom into humans. This usually causes immediate, intense pain, followed by swelling around the sting. An effective 'bush remedy' for the pain of

> **MULTIPLE MISERIES**
> Twenty stings from any species of bull ant are supposed to be fatal. This is hard to verify as most people don't hang around to get stung that many times.

a bull ant and other hymenoptera stings, is the common bracken. Break off and bend a stem back and forth. Rub the sap directly onto the site of the sting and the pain should rapidly disappear. Bracken is quite common in many parts of the Australian bush.

Bracken is quite common in the bush.

Wasps

Polistes *paper wasps attending young grubs in their cells. Sealed cells house metamorphosing grubs. Inset: A* Ropalidia *wasp.*

Not all wasps sting but many Australian wasps do and there have been several deaths from wasp stings, mainly due to allergic reactions. The ones that regularly cause problems are the social species that form papery nests, both native and introduced. Among the native wasps, *Ropalidia* and *Polistes* species are troublesome. So, too, are two introduced *Polistes* species and two introduced European wasps — *Vespula germanica* and *V. vulgaris*. The nests of these species are often found around houses or urban areas, so they are prone to disturbance by humans; their response is often aggressive.

Wasps' Nesting Habits

The multi-layered nests of European wasps are about the size of a loaf of bread or larger. They may be exposed, in a tree cavity or even underground. There are instances of people, having run over an underground nest entrance with a lawnmower, incurring mass stingings and even death. European wasps are also attracted to food and drink, so stings often occur around barbecues.

Ropalidia paper wasps are more docile species. Their papery nests typically hang vertically and the wasps seem sluggish and reluctant to take flight. Nevertheless, they will sting if someone brushes against the nest, which is often hidden in shrubs. *Polistes* paper wasps, both native and exotic, tend to build their nests with the cells in a horizontal plane. They are extremely territorial wasps: close proximity is often enough to trigger an attack.

If you want to remove a wasp nest but are allergic to wasp stings, either call in professional pest controllers or ask a non-allergic friend to remove it for you.

Honeybees

A European Honeybee collects pollen. Inset: Feral European Honeybees construct a hive in a fallen eucalypt log.

The humble introduced European Honeybee kills more people annually (about 25) than spiders and snakes combined. The reason for this is that many people are allergic to bee stings and what might cause only pain and swelling in one person can be a life-threatening experience for another.

European Honeybees are widespread throughout Australia and exist in both cultivated and feral hives in bushland and urban areas. The sting of this bee is barbed, so once embedded in a victim, it cannot be retracted; the bee that stings you dies as a result. So widespread are European Honeybees that most people think they are native.

Most of the 2000-plus native bee species are not aggressive and stings are rare. The social native bees have no sting at all, although some will resort to biting if trapped. The solitary natives do have a sting and, because it is not barbed, they can sting repeatedly.

Barbed Stings

Solitary bees rarely, if ever, defend their nests against humans. This is because each female can reproduce so she can always make a new nest rather than risk her life. Social species cannot reproduce unless they are the queen or drones. This means that each worker will defend her queen and nest with her life.

STINGLESS SAWFLIES

Sawflies, like ants, bees and wasps, are part of the hymenoptera group of insects but they are relatively primitive and none of their ovipositors have evolved into stingers, so you have nothing to fear from sawflies or their 'spitfire' larvae.

Ants

Bull ants (above) deliver powerful stings. Green Tree Ants (inset) repairing their nest — although edible, they can bite your lips!

There are possibly thousands of ant species in Australia. Some lack stingers but squirt formic acid from their abdomens as defence instead. Many others bite and sting, but the effects on humans are usually only temporary localised pain and irritation. Lawn ants, green-headed ants and some others can be a painful nuisance if trapped against skin or sat upon. These ants have hard bodies and so are difficult to crush. Being small, they are also not very obvious and may go unnoticed. The pain and associated swelling usually subsides in less than an hour. The recently introduced Red Fire Ant, although small, is aggressive and has a 'firey' painful sting.

Some Serious Ant Stings

More serious are the stings of bull ants, bulldog ants, soldier ants and jumping ants, which are aggressive, curious and have a very painful sting. Luckily these ants are usually solitary foragers but standing on a nest or disturbing one may precipitate a multiple attack.

Allergic reactions to ant stings have been recorded and severe reactions should be treated seriously. For milder reactions there are commercial preparations and 'bush remedies' to treat the pain (see page 39).

> ### BEING EATEN BY YOUR LUNCH
> The Green Tree Ant of tropical northern Australia has a pleasant citrus taste. Indigenous people crush them into water as a medicine or pluck them off branches as a snack. The head is held between finger and thumb and the ant's body is bitten off behind the head. Take care when doing this as the ants may bite your lips or tongue if you swallow them whole.

Stinging Caterpillars

Cup moths have some of the most beautifully coloured and patterned caterpillars but they usually sting if you touch them.

Watch out for 'hairy' caterpillars. The stings of some can be surprisingly sharp and both stings and rashes may ache for some time. Australia has several species that do this. They employ one of two mechanisms. They either have a set of hollow spiny bristles which, if you brush against them, transfer poison into your skin (envenomation), or a set of barbed hairs, some with venom and some without, break off the caterpillar and embed themselves into skin.

Cup moths and gum-leaf skeletonisers use this first method. The bristles of cup moths fold away in clusters or rosettes. When danger threatens, they become erect and can inflict a painful sting, often causing a broad, low weal. The gum-leaf skeletonisers have clumps of bristles down their backs that cause stings and weals if a person brushes against them.

Barbed and Embedded

With the second type of stinging caterpillar, barbed hairs are embedded in the skin on contact with the victim. Some species, however, have very brittle hairs that break free and blow about in the wind, causing skin irritation without even seeing the cause. Rashes and dermatitis commonly result from barbed caterpillar hairs. Furthermore, in order to protect their cocoons, many of these caterpillars incorporate these hairs into their constructions. Even cast skins can cause rashes. Moreover, the hairs can retain their capacity to irritate for several years, so even handling dead specimens or cocoons is not recommended.

RASH RELIEF
If you develop a rash after a caterpillar has left barbed hairs stuck in your skin, you can remove them with sticking plaster, sticky tape or fine forceps. Alternatively visit a beautician to get the area waxed: when the wax comes off, so too will the barbed hairs.

How Do Caterpillar Hairs Cause Stinging?

Processionary caterpillars have brittle hairs.

With 'envenomating hairs' the cause of the sting is easy to understand. The stiff hollow hairs or bristles pierce your skin and the venom within the hair, or venom injected from a gland at the hair's base, enters your body, causing pain in the process.

With 'non-envenomating hairs' it is a little harder to understand. The hairs are stiff, pointed and have barbs along their length. These barbs are angled so that once the hairs have penetrated your skin they are not just difficult to pull out, they often continue to work their way deeper in. The rash and pain comes from having irritating 'foreign matter' embedded in your flesh, in much the same way as a splinter causes pain and irritation.

How Can I Avoid Caterpillar Stings?

Wearing a long-sleeved shirt and gloves while working in areas where cup moth larvae are active will help prevent most stings. Avoid touching hairy caterpillars or leaning against tree trunks where these types of caterpillars are seen. Stay out of places where 'bag worms' or processionary caterpillars are active until they have become moths and flown away.

These caterpillars are so-named because they shelter in a silken 'bag' at night and travel in single file to new feeding areas in wattle trees by day. They have brittle hairs that break free and blow about in vast numbers. Anyone coming in contact with these drifting hairs, or leaning against branches that have been covered in hairs, may suffer great discomfort.

In parts of the Northern Territory, the caterpillars that feed on freshwater mangrove trees have these drifting hairs. They cause such irritation that nearby schools sometimes have to close until the problem passes.

A caterpillar trail. Large quantities of hairs from these caterpillars can get blown about in the wind and sting unsuspecting people.

Why Do Some Flies Bite?

The thick piercing mouthpart of a female March Fly can penetrate blue jeans.

In most species of biting fly it is only the breeding females that bite and feed on blood. The males and non-breeding females of these species, including many mosquitoes, usually feed on plant juices and nectar.

Breeding females need blood for the extra protein that it contains. Protein is helpful to egg development. The production of eggs requires a great deal of nourishment and animal protein is a particularly rich source of easily digestible material.

There are just a few fly species, such as stable flies, where both sexes feed only on blood at all times.

How Can I Avoid Fly Bites?

The easiest way to avoid the bites of flies is to apply some form of insect repellent to your skin. There are many effective commercial preparations, some based on tea-tree or eucalyptus oil. Tiger balm is also effective. Donning long sleeved tops, long trousers and socks helps to reduce the available flesh exposed to attack but many biting flies can bite through thin, and sometimes even thick, material.

For mosquitoes, citronella is a popular mossie deterrent: candles, joss sticks and skin oils are all readily available. In some areas only repellents containing DEET seem to be effective. Indigenous people of the Northern Territory recommend burning the insides of old termite mounds in the campfire.

A plethora of fly repellents are available.

Sandflies are small and can often penetrate mosquito netting. In areas where they occur, ask locals what they recommend.

Many biting flies are active during the day but mossies are most lively at dusk and at night. Sandflies are common in the early morning and late afternoon/early evening. Flies often occur seasonally and/or only at certain altitudes. Knowing the habits of particular species will help you to avoid them.

Biting Flies

The march fly is large and bites painfully but it is slow and easily swatted. Inset: A close-up of a march fly.

Biting flies of one type or another can be found throughout Australia. They come in a range of sizes and shapes from march flies that exceed 2 cm in length to miniscule sandflies at little over 1 mm. With the exception of mosquitoes, none of the Australian biting flies are known to carry disease.

A Variety of Biting Flies

Sandflies (or biting midges) are associated with coastal swamps and mangroves but are found inland in some areas. Usually tiny, they are unnoticeable in the twilight until they bite. Mainly an annoyance in warmer weather, some people have severe itching after bites but locals often develop an immunity.

Stable flies are often found around horses. Superficially resembling ordinary houseflies, their bite leaves no doubt about their identity. They are more common in warmer weather and in temperate to tropical parts of Australia.

March flies are more abundant in summer and in the tropics but can be found almost anywhere, including the Australian Alps. Large, clumsy and easy to swat, their bites are painful.

Black flies can be a problem in inland areas prone to summer floods. After the warm rains, they sometimes hatch out in large numbers.

> **IN THE SWIM**
> Not all fly larvae look like maggots. Black flies and mosquitoes breed in water and their larvae, called wrigglers, swim. Dark coloured, with obvious heads, they breathe through syphons in their 'tails' and look completely un-maggot like (see opposite).

Mosquitoes

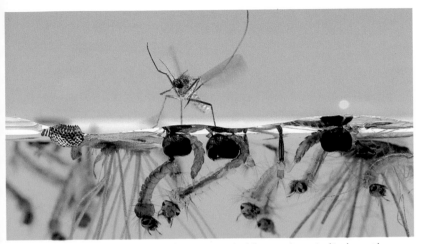

All the life cycle stages of a mosquito — egg, larva, pupa and adult — can be seen in this photograph.

Mosquitoes occur throughout Australia. There are nearly 300 different species here. Adults usually feed on plant juices. Most feeding is at twilight or at night. Certain species, however, also feed during the day, particularly in damp shady areas or on overcast days. When females are ready to breed some species seek out a blood meal. Different species choose different hosts. Several species happily feed on humans. The female lays her eggs in still water. Some species choose small stagnant sites like water in the saucer of a pot plant; others prefer larger sites, such as mangrove swamps.

CHAIN OF EVENTS
Mosquitoes must catch a disease in order to pass it on to you. This transmission is often via infected saliva, which the mosquito pumps into you to keep your blood flowing smoothly. The source of infection for the mosquito is usually another person with the disease.

Diseases Carried by Mosquitoes

Although mosquito bites are irritating, they usually heal after a couple of days and cause no lasting damage. Several Australian species, however, sometimes transmit disease. For example, dengue fever, Australian encephalitis, Ross River virus and Barmah Forest virus can be all be transmitted by mosquitoes. These diseases are widely distributed outside their place-name vicinities.

Up until 1981, malaria was present in the Australian tropics. A careful ongoing control program seems to have eradicated it but just next door — in Papua New Guinea — malaria remains rife. Most modern cases of malaria in Australia now arrive from overseas. Nevertheless, we still have the mosquito species that carries this disease, even in Sydney, so an outbreak is always a possibility.

Scorpions

Scorpions belong to the group that includes spiders and mites. Those living in Australia may be 2–10 cm long. Recognisable by their eight legs, two front claws and the curled tail bearing their venomous sting, they are sometimes confused with the harmless earwig, which has six legs, no front claws but pincers on its tail.

A scorpion on the prowl and ready for lunch.

Scorpions feed on insects and other invertebrates, which they usually incapacitate by stinging first. They hunt at night, usually hiding by the day beneath rocks, logs or in burrows. When camping, it is wise to shake out shoes and clothing before putting them on.

Only two deaths from scorpion stings have been recorded in Australia. While they are not regarded as a serious danger, they can deliver a painful sting. The smaller species seem to inflict the worst stings. Because of potential allergic reactions, seek medical help if symptoms increase or persist.

SCORPION GHOSTS
Under UV light, many scorpions fluoresce with a ghostly green or violet light. Scorpion hunters walk around likely areas at night carrying a UV light to reveal the ghostly glow of scorpions.

Banded centipedes can give painful bites.

Centipedes

Centipedes are found across Australia but only large species in the family Scolopendridae present any real problem. Others are mostly small and unlikely to bite humans effectively. Large centipedes, up to 14 cm long, live in bushland and urban areas. Active, rapid and predatory, they feed on insects, spiders and even small reptiles. One desert centipede was witnessed catching and devouring a small snake larger than itself.

Centipedes are nocturnal. During the day they hide under rocks, logs or in burrows. At night they hunt by following scent trails. They may enter houses and crawl inside boots, shoes, sleeping bags and clothing on the ground. Shake out shoes and clothing if there is a chance a centipede dropped in for a visit. Centipedes have been known to nip unprotected toes and fingers, mistaking them for prey. Their bite is very painful and, while no deaths have occurred in Australia, they have been recorded overseas, although they are rare. Despite their ferocious reputation, females are maternal. They brood their eggs and young until they are old enough to disperse.

Most mites are too small to see with the naked eye. This 'giant' Red Velvet Mite (at 3mm) is a harmless scavenger.

Mites

Mites are related to spiders and have eight legs as adults. They live in a myriad habitats: some inhabit soil, others vegetation. They have rasping and sucking mouthparts that often damage plants but only a few species are detrimental to human health. Most mites are tiny (1–2 mm long) and difficult to see.

Best known perhaps are the dust mites that lurk everywhere in our homes. They cause respiratory problems for asthma sufferers when they, or their droppings, are inhaled. Some mites living across Australia's tropical north transmit scrub typhus.

Another disease caused by mites is scabies. Scabies mites take up residence by burrowing under the skin, creating unpleasant rashes that itch mercilessly. Occasionally bird mites mistake humans as a suitable host, leaving extremely itchy spots where they bite us. It is small consolation to sufferers to know that such mites die after feeding on the wrong hosts.

Ticks

Tick bites are most unpleasant and can carry diseases. The most severely infested tick areas are along the eastern edge of Australia. Ticks cling to vegetation along paths in bushland or grasses, waiting for a warm-blooded creature to pass by. They then drop onto their victims, wade through any hair and bury their jaws deep into flesh to suck on their host's blood. Adult females require protein from the blood to produce eggs.

Tick bites in humans can result in severe itching, headaches, swollen lymph nodes and pain around the

A paralysis tick, swollen from a recent blood meal.

site of the bite. In some species, the toxin they pump into the bloodstream can cause paralysis. While rare in adults, this is a very real risk for children and is quite common among domestic pets.

Remove embedded ticks as soon as possible. This requires a pair of tweezers and a steady hand. Once well positioned, pluck the tick out carefully without squeezing in more toxin. A good soak in a bath of bicarb is another means of removal. As a last resort, shave the infected area, thereby cutting the tick in half.

What Diseases Do Bloodsuckers Carry?

*I*n Australia, at least nine diseases are known to be transmitted to humans by blood-sucking invertebrates. Mosquitoes carry five diseases (see page 47), ticks carry three and mites one. Having said that, mosquito-, tick- and mite-borne diseases are rarely fatal if medical aid is sought early.

Native mites of tropical northern Australia carry a bacteria-like micro-organism that causes scrub typhus. The mites pick up the disease from infected rodents in the forests and grasslands.

Some ticks transmit diseases from hosts such as possums and bandicoots to humans resulting in symptoms similar to the North American Lyme disease. Tick typhus and spotted fevers are also tick dangers all of which may cause varying amounts of fevers, rashes, joint pains, flu-like symptoms, and swollen glands.

Mosquitoes can carry more than one disease at a time.

Mosquitoes also carry diseases that affect our pets. Heartworm, for example, is a common killer of dogs but preventative medication for this is available.

Why Do Bloodsuckers Carry Disease?

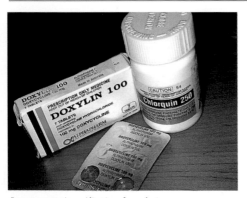

Some preventative medications for malaria.

*B*lood-sucking vectors (disease carriers) do not intentionally spread disease when they bite people. They are only after their next meal. The organisms that cause the disease are actually hitchhiking a ride with the parasite as it travels from one infected person or animal to a new uninfected one.

As a vector bites an infected animal, it also sucks up any disease organisms living in the blood. When it bites another animal, the disease organisms are transmitted via the bite, to the new host. Since these organisms often must bore their way through the vector's gut and into its salivary glands, the vector is often as afflicted by the disease as is the person who receives its bite.

How Do Leeches Feed?

*A*ustralia has freshwater and land leeches that will bite humans. Water leeches sometimes attack waders and swimmers in slow-flowing or still water but land leeches are more commonly encountered.

Land leeches usually inhabit damp or humid places, such as rainforests and gullies, where they actively seek out hosts for blood meals. Long and thin, one end often remains attached on the ground while the other waves around trying to pick up the heat of a warm-blooded animal. It then attaches itself to the 'animal' and finds a hidden spot on the skin to feed. In humans the inside of a shoe or sock or under a watchband is choice. It snips the skin with its jaws, leaving a characteristic V- or Y-shaped cut, and pumps anti-coagulant in its saliva into its victim to prevent the blood from clotting. Once full, the leech drops off its host and finds a quiet spot to digest its meal.

This leech is swollen from a blood meal.

Itching and Bleeding

Bites may bleed and itch for some time after the leech has gone. With water leeches, washing the bite and wiping it dry with a towel is often enough to stop the itching and bleeding. Land-leech wounds may itch for days and leave a bloody scab. Wash the wound and apply calamine lotion. A sturdy sticking plaster will protect the bite from opening up again. In most cases time is the only thing that will stop the itch.

DR BLOOD
Leeches are used for medical purposes. Water leeches are best as they cause less itching and post-op bleeding. In Wales, medicinal leeches are 'farmed' to send to hospitals worldwide. They are used to keep the blood flowing in the tissue of re-attached severed appendages, such as fingers or ears, until they can heal.

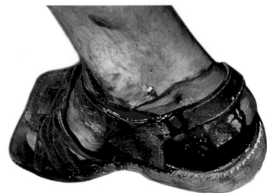

Leech bites often bleed freely for some time after the leech has dropped off its host.

Cane Toads

Cane Toads are wreaking havoc with the native frog populations.
Inset: White poison oozes from the glands sitting behind the toad's eyes.

TESTING TOADS
The toxins in Cane Toad skin may have benefits after all. They are being investigated for their apparent anti-fungal and anti-bacterial properties.

This 15 cm-long warty frog was introduced early last century in an attempt to control two native beetles that were eating sugarcane foliage and threatening the industry. The measure was a total failure. Not only was the non-climbing toad unable to reach the beetles, the toad itself rapidly became a pest, eating many native animals and poisoning others that tried to eat it. Covered in poison glands, its powerful array of toxins can kill. Many would-be predators die after their first taste. With little to slow its spread, the toad has dispersed and it has even turned up as far south as Sydney. Although there are no confirmed reports of it breeding so far south, this may just be a matter of time.

A Terrible Toxin

The skin toxin can only be squirted under pressure, by striking or stepping on a toad. If toxin gets on your skin, wash it off immediately. Sometimes the poison just exudes onto the toad's skin. The greatest danger is getting the toxin in your eyes or mouth. If this occurs, flush with water and seek medical aid. Some harmless or rare native frogs are often mistaken for Cane Toads, but they lack the combination of large glands on the back of the neck and ridges of skin running from nose to eye. Check with wildlife authorities if unsure. Cane Toad spawn appears in strings like a beaded necklace, so it is easily recognised.

Funnel-web Spiders

A funnel-web displays its typical threat pose. Inset: One of the tree-dwelling funnel-webs.

Funnel-webs are large, robust spiders, up to 6 cm long. Their head and legs are usually a shiny black. If disturbed, they rear up in an alarmingly aggressive threat pose which means 'leave me alone'. You are well advised to do so. Funnel-webs prefer damp, cool conditions. Most species shelter and build webs beneath rocks, logs or other cover and are rarely seen, but a few live in trees. Wandering males may fall into swimming pools where they can survive for many hours, or they may enter houses. Do not handle even seemingly dead specimens, be sure to shake out shoes left lying on the floor, check swimming pools before jumping in and don't wander in the dark without shoes.

Funnel-webs are distributed throughout eastern Australia from Gladstone in Queensland to the Eyre Peninsula in South Australia, as well as in Tasmania. The Sydney Funnel-web is found as far as Lithgow in the west and from Newcastle to Nowra north to south.

A Serious Threat to Safety

This is perhaps the most frightening animal in Australia. Its bite is often deadly and, due to human disturbance of its natural habitat, close encounters are frequent. Come summer and autumn, male funnel-webs leave their burrows and go walkabout in search of females with which to mate. Although nocturnal, it is often at this time of year that trouble arises.

Since 1927, when records began to be kept, 14 deaths have been attributed to the Sydney Funnel-web alone and there are at least 36 other species of funnel-webs thought to exist.

The handsome male Red-headed Mouse Spider.

Mouse Spiders

Neither a mouse catcher, nor mouse-like, this spider's name is misleading. Being only 1 to 2.5 cm long, it is not thought to be as dangerous as a funnel-web but it is active by day and, when threatened, will rear up and spread its jaws impressively. Although few bites have been recorded, they should be taken seriously, especially when children are about. One bite was reported as responding well to funnel-web antivenom.

Mouse spiders are found almost everywhere in Australia. They live in burrows in bushland and are quite common in urban gardens. Females are rarely seen as they spend most of their lives in their burrows, which are carefully camouflaged and fitted with trapdoor lids. In the warmer months, however, males are often encountered as, like male funnel-webs, they are out and about looking for females.

Females look superficially like short-legged, squat funnel-webs. Males can be quite distinctive, some species having red heads and bluish abdomens, while others have a conspicuous silvery white patch on the top of the abdomen.

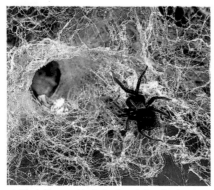

A Black House-spider in its funnel-shaped web.

Black House-spiders

These spiders are found throughout Australia and, as their name suggests, they are common around houses and buildings, especially around windows. They are often accidentally transported in building materials and it is not uncommon to see cars and other vehicles with a resident population of Black House-spiders around the radiator grill and bumper bars. Their distinctive funnel-shaped web often causes concern among people who suspect they might be funnel-web spiders, but the bite of this species is painful rather than dangerous. They are also much smaller, with the female measuring only 1.8 cm and males around 1 cm. Of perhaps greater concern is the fact that a population of house spiders will usually attract White-tailed Spiders, which feed on them.

A Red-back Spider sucks body fluids from its prey.

Red-back Spider

Closely related to the American Black Widow Spider, the Red-back Spider can be found all over Australia and is quite common around human habitation. Males are patterned in red, black and white. Being tiny (body length under 3 mm) they are unlikely to pierce the skin and so pose no threat. The larger female, however, is a very distinctive black and red and about 1.4 cm long; she can deliver a very painful bite and may be considered dangerous to those with an allergic reaction to the venom. If in doubt, seek medical advice.

Red-back Spiders often build their webs in rubbish heaps and building materials. They seem to prefer drier conditions rather than damp or humid ones. Their diet includes various insects and other invertebrates that become tangled in their webs.

> **DUNNY SPIDER**
>
> Red-backs often live in secluded spots in or around pit toilets, where insect food is plentiful. The song about the Red-back on the toilet seat was right, except that it would be more likely to be underneath the seat than on it.

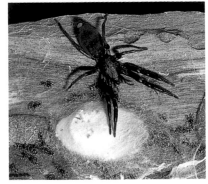

A female White-tailed Spider attends her young.

White-tailed Spider

The Australia-wide range of the White-tailed Spider closely mirrors that of its favourite food item, the Black House-spider. These spiders eat other spiders, too, but their strategy of tickling the webs of Black House-spiders to draw the resident within striking range seems particularly effective.

The male is only about 1.2 cm long while the larger female reaches 2 cm. Neither sex builds a real web or silken home of its own unless moulting or guarding an egg sac but they roam about — particularly in places where house spiders abound. This brings them in contact with people, who often find them crawling on the floor and occasionally…in the bed.

Controversy abounds as to whether this spider's venom causes ulceration and skin death around the bite area. Certainly it has been implicated in some cases, but in others the type of spider was never verified. Furthermore, some people suffer no such effects. It is possible that bacteria infect the bite area and it is these that actually cause the problem.

LARGE WATER ANIMALS

Which Large Water Animals Are Dangerous?

Divers beware, poking fingers into the mouth of a Mosaic Moray Eel is not recommended.

*M*ost water animals that do us harm live in the ocean rather than in freshwater. An exception, and a surprising one at that, is the shy Platypus. Only by handling the male Platypus can a person come in contact with its venomous spurs. They present absolutely no danger to swimmers, provided they are left alone. Unfortunately the same cannot be said of the Saltwater Crocodile of northern Australia.

Top of most people's list of dangerous seawater animals would have to be the sharks. There are indeed several species you need to be wary of but the Great White Shark probably has the greatest claim to notoriety.

Many creatures living in Australian waters have developed powerful defence capabilities and inevitably some encounters do go wrong. Having said this, it cannot be emphasised enough what fun it is discovering the world of the ocean. By learning a bit about the animals that live there, you will be well prepared for what to expect. Most marine creatures will leave you alone provided you do the same.

How Can a Platypus Harm You?

*W*e don't usually think of mammals as being venomous animals but, strange to believe, our beloved egg-laying Platypus is one. Mind you, this only applies to the male, which has on his hind legs a pair of spurs that are connected to venom glands.

The Platypus will only spur people who try to handle it. If an angler accidentally catches a Platypus, experts recommend wrapping it firmly in a coat or bag before unhooking or disentangling it from a net or trap. Otherwise call an animal rescue service.

Platypus venom in the human bloodstream causes deep pain and a swelling that lasts for some time. Dogs have reputedly been killed by this venom and, although there have been no human deaths, medical assistance is recommended. To stop the pain, powerful nerve-blocking painkillers are sometimes used. The more conventional anti-inflammatory agents have little effect.

The Platypus's venomous spurs are tucked into the base of its hind feet.

FIGHTING FEET
The Platypus' front feet have sharp, broad claws to help it dig and also scramble over rough ground. When in the water, the webbing that was bent back across its palm unfolds. It extends well beyond the claws, equipping the animal with powerful front paddles. The male's hind feet bare the venomous spurs.

Are Crocodiles Dangerous?

*Y*es. Saltwater Crocodiles have attacked and eaten people both in Australia and overseas. Since 1971 hunting crocodiles has been prohibited and the size, abundance and lack of fear in these animals has increased.

In addition, further human settlement in previously sparsely inhabited areas has led to the potential for more frequent contact between humans and crocodiles. Despite this situation, crocodile

This Saltwater Crocodile lies motionless and well camouflaged at the water's edge, awaiting unwary prey.

attacks remain rare, with an average of one death every second year.

Sizing Up Crocs

Of the two living species in Australia, the Freshwater Crocodile is relatively small and probably only a danger to anglers who accidently hook one or to people trying to corner or catch one. The Saltwater Crocodile, however, is the world's largest living crocodile and mature adults can be considered human-eaters (given the chance).

How Can I Avoid a Crocodile Attack?

*O*ne important recommendation is not to swim or wade in rivers or estuaries that are thought to be frequented by crocodiles. This includes most rivers, fresh or brackish, in the Top End of the Northern Territory, north Queensland and northern Western Australia. Crocodile warning signs are not always posted — if in doubt, don't risk it. Usually local residents can tell you where the

DINOS FOR DINNER
Some prehistoric crocodiles (like Deinosuchus of North America) grew up to 15 m and probably fed on dinosaurs and other megafauna.

safe swimming holes are.

There are other important ways to avoid crocodiles. Don't follow well-used tracks to the water's edge in croco-

A Saltwater Crocodile moves stealthily into position before the surprise attack.

dile country, particularly in the early morning or late evening. Don't camp on a site too close to the water's edge. There have been attacks on people, and dogs have been taken when chained too close to crocodile habitat. Don't fill the 'billy' from the same spot at the same time each day — crocodiles are keen observers of behaviour patterns in their prey.

Platypus

An adept swimmer, the Platypus finds food with its bill.

EXPERT DETECTORS

Platypus swim underwater with their eyes and ears closed, yet they easily locate their prey as they fossick along the bottom. Their rubbery bills are sensitive to the minute electrical fields and discharges that all animals give off during movement.

Platypuses are more common than most people realise but draining or damming of waterways, pollution and even competition from introduced trout may affect their numbers. They inhabit permanent waterways ranging from fast mountain streams to slow meandering rivers, lakes and billabongs on the eastern edge of Australia from Cooktown in the north, following the coast and ranges south to Victoria, Tasmania and the eastern edge of South Australia. Shy and active mainly during the twilight hours, they are not often seen. Freshwater anglers, canoeists and people who frequent waterways early in the morning are most likely to see them. Sadly, many are accidentally caught in fishing nets or crayfish traps and they drown quickly. Always leave an 'air access' space at the top of your traps to prevent this.

Venomous Spurs

The spurs on the hind legs of the male Platypus are used against both predators and any rival Platypus. Sometimes overly aggressive males have been known to kill large fish and frogs during the breeding season. Interestingly, the amount of venom produced varies during the year, reaching its maximum through the breeding season in spring. This is thought to help males defend their territories against other males. Their diet consists of frogs, tadpoles, shrimp, crayfish, worms and aquatic insects.

Crocodiles

Saltwater Crocodiles (above) grow to 7 metres and sometimes eat humans. Freshwater Crocodiles (inset), luckily, are too small.

You need only worry about crocodiles if you are in the hot, humid northern parts of Australia. There are two species. The Freshwater Crocodile lives only in the freshwater habitats of far northern Australia. Growing to little more than 3 metres, it is not a serious threat to human life although lacerations can occur if the animal is restrained, feels threatened or is hooked by an angler.

The Saltwater Crocodile inhabits rivers, billabongs, estuaries, mangroves and even the open ocean around northern Australia, New Guinea and South-eastern Asia. Large animals can reach up to 7 metres in length. Such heavyweights are enormously powerful in the water and while their usual fare consists of birds, reptiles and fish, they sometimes take wallabies and even Water Buffalo, so the odd human makes a nice change. They normally stalk their prey by stealth, moving just beneath the surface of the water.

GENTLE MUMS

Crocodiles may seem fierce to us but females are capable of great gentleness when they transport their young broods in their mouths. Despite numerous sharp teeth, the young remain completely unscathed.

Breeding and Feeding

Females of both crocodile species lay eggs in a nest, which they defend until the young hatch. They then keep watch until they can fend for themselves.

Both species may feed by day but are more active at night. Freshwater Crocodiles eat mainly fish but take other small vertebrates if the opportunity arises. The Salties take fish and small vertebrates when young but adults can manage prey up to the size of a Water Buffalo.

Sea Snakes

Both Stokes Sea Snake (above) and the Yellow Bellied Sea Snake (inset) inhabit Australian waters and are venomous.

Sea snakes are recognised by their scaly bodies and paddle-shaped tails. Of the two sea-snake families, one is wholly aquatic and gives birth to live young at sea, while the other—a group known as the sea kraits—lays eggs and must sometimes come onto land to deposit them.

Various species of sea snake are found around Australia's coastline, with the exception of the far south and Tasmania; even in these cooler waters, on rare occasions seas snakes occur, swept offcourse by ocean currents. Healthy sea snakes are usually found offshore in the tropics and are frequently seen around coral reefs, while sick or injured ones regularly wash up on beaches.

LONG LUNGS

Sea snakes (and indeed most other snakes) only have one functional lung. Possibly there isn't enough room in those long skinny bodies for two working lungs. To compensate, the left lung is longer than usual for a reptile of this size, so the snake is able to get as much oxygen as it requires.

Staying Clear of Sea Snakes

Many sea snakes have highly toxic venom but the fangs are usually short, so 'dry bites' are common. Fatalities are rare but bites must be treated seriously. One species found in Australian waters, *Enhydrina schistosa*, kills more people annually than any other, yet neither it nor any other sea snake has caused a death in Australia to date.

Victims elsewhere are usually fishing hands and trawler operators sorting out their catch. Sea snakes are sometimes curious and will investigate divers; they are completely harmless provided they are left alone. Unrestrained sea snakes in the water rarely bite. Only if they are handled, attacked, severely buffeted in the water, hooked on a fishing line or tangled in nets will they bite.

Eels

Although normally shy, moray eels like these Green Morays can inflict serious lacerations. Inset: A freshwater eel.

On occasion moray, conger and freshwater eels have all bitten unwary humans. Eels can be found right around the coast, as well as in major freshwater rivers, streams, creeks, swamps and dams. Anglers regularly catch eels. As with other animals, the truly wild ones are wary and usually shy away from human contact. Where people, such as divers, feed them, this wariness disappears and they can become more aggressive in their attempts to elicit food. Attacks can sometimes occur as a result of aggression or confusion over where the food ends and human hands begin. Indeed a moray eel can easily mistake the pale, waving palms and soles of a swimmer's hands and feet for a fish.

> **GYPSY LIFESTYLE**
> Freshwater eels spawn in the ocean and the larval eels travel vast distances back to their parents' freshwater habitats in Australia. Baby eels or elvers can cross wet ground at night to reach isolated farm dams. They can even scale waterfalls and dam walls.

Freshwater Eels

Freshwater eel bites are usually minor, but a hungry eel mistaking a human finger or toe for food will sometimes spin on its own axis trying to twist off a morsel of flesh. A moray eel may bite and then form a knot with its body and try to pull its head through to tear off the bitten piece. The bites may result in serious lacerations, which, in the water, can lead to severe loss of blood. There is also a danger of septicaemia after a bite. Even the recently severed head of an eel can bite, so be cautious when unhooking them.

How Dangerous Are Sharks?

Although relatively harmless, this gentle giant should not be harrassed for the safety of both the diver and the shark as they can cause abrasions.

*T*he short answer is not very. You are probably in far more danger of being in an aircraft crash than you are of being attacked by a shark. There are more than 166 species of shark in Australian waters and most of them are too small to consider humans as suitable prey. This is not to say that you can take liberties with sharks.

As a general rule, the larger the shark the more dangerous it is to humans. The enormous plankton-feeding Whale Shark, however, is an exception. It is a docile shark. At Ningaloo Reef, off the south-western coast of Western Australia, people dive to swim with these gentle giants. Provided they do not venture too close, it can be a wonderful experience.

At the other end of the scale are the whaler sharks, the Tiger Sharks and the Great Whites. These are species to be extremely wary of.

What Eats Sharks?

*P*eople eat far more sharks than sharks eat people. The 'flake' you buy as fish and chips is usually shark, and shark-fin soup is very popular in some parts of the world. Sadly, as a result of their slow rate of breeding and low fertility, shark species that are commercially fished are becoming quite scarce and several shark fisheries have already collapsed.

In addition, some shark species eat other sharks, and many predatory fish may include any shark smaller than themselves in their diet. Killer Whales and other, small-

Anyone for shark and chips?

er, toothed whales, such as dolphins, may also eat small sharks. Some molluscs feed on shark eggs and, in some sharks that give birth to live young, the first baby to develop in the womb turns cannibalistic. It devours its slower siblings until only one or two offspring survive to be born.

Are Shark Nets Effective?

*S*hark nets are strung across the entrance to many popular Australia beaches. These nets catch not just the potentially dangerous sharks but harmless sharks, turtles, stingrays, and on occasion sea mammals like Dugongs and dolphins. Shark attacks have certainly dropped considerably since their use, but then so have shark numbers. Education and shark-spotting lifeguards have also proved effective means of reducing shark attacks, so

Several Sydney beaches have fully enclosed shark nets to protect swimmers from possible shark attack.

the fewer attacks may just be a result of these, rather than the netting.

Some shark species must continually swim forward to ensure the flow of water over their gills. It is from this flowing water that the sharks are able to extract oxygen for breathing. If this forward motion ceases, as it inevitably must once a shark is entangled in a net, then oxygen ceases to be available to the shark and it will drown. Many conservation groups are calling for bans on beach netting for this reason.

How Can I Avoid Shark Attack?

*T*here are several commonsense measures you can take to avoid shark attack. Firstly, heed warning signs about sharks. Secondly, don't swim in turbid water or at dawn or dusk. These are times when sharks may be actively seeking a meal.

Swimming or diving near seal colonies or around dense schools of fish are far more risky situations for a shark attack than swimming at spots where 'shark food' is less concentrated. In such circumstances take safety precautions, such as having companions to watch out for you. When spearfishing, never go alone and don't carry your catch on your belt. Lastly, you are asking for trouble if you get too close to sharks or if you tease or torment them. Hand-feeding wild sharks is an absolute no-no.

If you want to play it really safe, only swim in enclosed beach-swimming areas.

Hungry sharks feed among sea lions and large shoals of fish, so keep clear of these.

SCARCE SHARKS
Many shark species have recently become rare. Overfishing, trophy hunting, pollution and the disappearance of food have all taken their toll. A low rate of reproduction makes sharks susceptible to overfishing. Also, many species take several years to reach maturity before they start breeding. Some species, such as the Grey Nurse Shark, are now so rare that they are protected by law.

Tiger Shark

Potentially the most dangerous shark in the world.

This shark can move very fast. It is recorded as potentially the world's most dangerous shark, having attacked and/or eaten many people. It has a broad dietary range, feeding on sea mammals, seabirds, turtles, fish, squid, carrion and even indigestible garbage.

It instinctively homes in on disturbances in the water and groups have been known to congregate at places where food is plentiful or is expected to appear at certain times, such as at sea-bird rookeries during fledging time.

Tiger Sharks can grow to 5 m long. They are widely distributed around the tropics, their range extending down the east and west coasts of Australia. They have broad heads and dark eyes, and although their distinctive banding varies from conspicuous to faint, it is nearly always present.

A curious species, these sharks will sometimes approach divers to investigate them and then swim off. Sometimes shy, they may wait hours before biting even a dead animal — but don't rely on this.

Whitetip Reef Shark

The Whitetip Reef Shark is harmless unless provoked.

The Whitetip Reef Shark grows to 2 m. It is commonly seen in tropical Australian waters. It is sometimes found asleep in a sea cave waiting for evening, during which time it becomes more active and does most of its feeding. This species is not considered a dangerous shark and is generally reasonably approachable. However, it is included here because, like wobbegongs and other

approachable sharks, it is sometimes teased, speared or otherwise tormented by curious divers. Under these circumstances this shark may well bite and it can cause serious lacerations. The moral of the story is 'let sleeping sharks lie'.

Because the Whitetip Reef Shark is sluggish by day and easy to get close to, a great many photographs have been taken of it. It is also frequently seen in tropical oceanariums.

Bronze Whaler

Two Australian whaler sharks have been caught with human remains inside them, and other fatalities have been attrib-

This whaler is potentially dangerous in southern waters.

uted to this species. What makes this shark so potentially dangerous is its habit of feeding in shallow water and estuaries (sometimes in turbid conditions), where people may be encountered. Both inshore and off the coast its quarry is a variety of fish and squid.

While many of its relatives prefer tropical waters, the Bronze Whaler is more commonly found around the southern half of Australia. It can grow to 3 m long, has a long nose, small eyes and a noticeable bronzy sheen.

> ### NAME-CALLING
> Whaler sharks got their common name from the days of commercial whaling. As whales were being brought in for processing these sharks would attack the bodies. They even followed the whaling boats out to sea on the off chance of a free meal.

Great White Shark

Perhaps the most famous shark, the Great White grows up to 6 m long and is widespread in the subtropical and temperate waters of the world. Most often seen in coastal areas, particularly near seal and sea lion colonies, it is also found out at sea.

Despite its reputation, attacks on people are rare. It is more a human 'biter' than 'eater'. Although serious or

The Great White is famous for its predatory nature.

fatal for the victim, attacks on humans are usually a case of mistaken identity. Once 'tasted', people are usually rejected.

Given the public and scientific interest, it is perhaps surprising that records of small specimens are quite rare and that breeding grounds and mating details are virtually unknown.

Great Whites are apparently good to eat and their thick, tough skin makes sturdy leather. Overfishing has caused an alarming drop in their numbers and in many areas this species is now protected.

Interestingly this shark's body temperature is usually slightly higher than the surrounding water. This enables it to feed and remain active in temperate waters but banishes it from the tropics because of the risk of overheating.

Which Fish Use Electric Shock Treatment?

*N*umbfishes and torpedo rays are all electric rays; that is they use 'shock treatment' to stun their prey and predators. If divers touch them they are at risk of being mistaken for predators; if shocked they may loose consciousness and drown. Anyone accidentally standing on an electric ray may also expect to be treated as a predator, as indeed may anyone touching them, unhooking them from a line or spearing them.

The Tasmanian Numbfish can electrocute humans.

The electric charge used for the shock is stored under the skin near the head of these rays, in a pair of large curved organs filled with jelly-like material. This storage material is actually modified muscle tissue that has lost its ability to contract. The lower surface of the ray is negative while the top surface is positive, so the discharge passes from one to the other causing a shock in the immediate vicinity. The charge is stored. The first shock is the most powerful. Subsequent shocks diminish in intensity until the ray must recharge. In order to recharge, as with other muscles, these 'storage muscles' require rest and energy.

Shocks can occur out of water. Anglers have reported shocks travelling up wet fishing lines. Even people pouring water over them or urinating on these fish have been shocked. Spear fishers with metal spears would certainly be well advised to avoid these fish.

Spear fishers, beware electric rays.

Is It Possible to See With Electricity?

*Y*es. Electric rays not only stun or catch prey with their electricity, they also 'see' their surroundings with it. Some electric fish, in fact, use their electricity for no other purpose than to find their way, their food and even their mates.

The fish give off small discharges of electricity to create an electrical field around

A SHOCKING LIFE
Electric rays are often afflicted with marine leeches. Strangely, these parasites seem to suffer no ill effects, although they must get the full brunt of any shocks the rays deliver.

Stargazers use electricity to detect food.

them. Any object within that field will distort it slightly, depending upon what it is made of. Rocks, sand and other materials that conduct electricity very poorly cause the field to distort around the object, while material that conducts electricity well causes the field to distort towards the object. Living animals are good conductors of electricity and so if they enter the field, they cause it to distort towards themselves.

Electric fish can detect these distortions and that is how they find their food, friends and predators. Some are so efficient they can find food in places other fish cannot see. Other fish can even 'talk' to one another in small electrical pulses. Who needs eyes when you can rely on electricity?

Who Are the Scorpionfish?

*T*hey are a family of fish that have earned their name from the venomous fin spines that all members of the family bear along their backs. Some also have venomous spines on their heads, gill covers and fins.

Scorpionfish are predators. Althought skilled at stalking or ambushing prey, most are rather slow at swimming away from danger. Their poisonous spines therefore are a defence mechanism against larger predators.

Among their number are the stonefish and the butterfly cods (page 71), both sea fish. Also in the scorpionfish family is the little-known Bullrout that inhabits fresh water (see page 92).

The sharp-tipped venomous spines of a stonefish can kill a human.

How Do I Avoid Being Stung or Shocked?

Stonefish may lie unseen in the shallows so rubber-soled shoes can save you a lot of pain.

*R*ubber-soled shoes and rubber gloves are useful for avoiding the effects of electric fish. When diving, always go with a companion — if you get shocked or stung underwater, help will be nearby. If you have to handle known or suspected members of the scorpionfish family, be sure to wear thick gloves. Wear stout footwear when travelling in shallow water around estuaries, reefs and rocks. When advancing through the water, a shuffling gait helps warn the fish of your approach.

Electric Rays

The numbfishes and torpedo rays are like other true rays except, instead of having a protective spike in their tail, they defend themselves and subdue their prey with a powerful electric shock. They are found throughout Australia's coastal waters except in the far north.

These 'flattened' fish have oblong bodies with smallish eyes on the top and mouths

The shocking Common or Short-tailed Numbfish.

FATAL LURE
The spiracle behind the eye of a buried common numbfish resembles a tubeworm and it may be used to attract prey close enough to be shocked and eaten.

on the bottom. They lie in ambush, half buried in the sandy, muddy bottoms of shallow or deep seawater. Here they wait for passing fish or crustaceans which they shock with jolts of 200 volts or more. Electric rays are all slow swimmers and for good reason — they do not need to swim quickly. They cruise along the sea bed using their tails and undulating their side flaps. For treatment of a shocked victim, see page 95.

Stingrays

Species in various stingray families are found all around the Australian coast, including estuarine areas. Like their relatives the sharks, they have a skeleton of cartilage and tiny tooth-like structures covering their skin called denticles, instead of scales. The males also bear shark-like 'claspers'. Also like sharks, some ray species lay eggs and some give birth

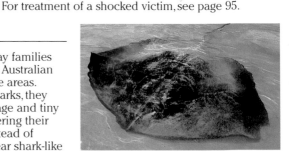

If provoked, large stingrays can cause serious injury.

to live young. Rays and sharks have no swim bladder to give them buoyancy and so they will sink if they stop swimming.

Stingrays are curious and may approach divers. Most common species are equipped with barbed spikes in their tails as protection from predators, such as sharks. Stingrays are usually not dangerous unless speared or grappled with. Of greater danger is the possibility of accidentally stepping on one buried in the sand at low tide, even in very shallow water.

If tormented, they may swing the barbed spike into the 'attacker'. The spike is brittle and often coated with venom. It frequently breaks off in the wound, causing considerable pain and swelling. Even baby stingrays being untangled from fishing nets or hooks can sting. A large ray can cause very painful lacerations that may be serious, or even fatal.

Stonefish are well camouflaged, so watch your step!

Stonefish

Stonefish are 20–30 cm long members of the scorpionfish family. They range along the northern coast of Australia, lurking in rocky, muddy, estuarine and reef habitats. These fish resemble algae-coated rocks. So effective is their comouflage that potential prey, such as smaller fish, are unaware of their presence. Once in range, these clumsy, sluggish stonefish suddenly 'inhale' their agile prey.

UGLY FOOD
Many species of scorpionfish are edible but anglers must take care when cleaning them as some species can still deliver a painful sting.

Stonefish have 13 spines on their backs that contain a very powerful toxin for use in defence. Their stings can be deadly to humans and several fatalities have been recorded.

Always wear stout footwear when wading in stonefish habitats. Being stung underwater is particularly dangerous as victims can easily drown while overcome by pain. The good news is that there is an antivenom available, so seek medical aid immediately if stung.

Butterfly Cods

Butterfly Cods are beautiful but encounters can be painful.

These spectacular fish have striking striped colour patterns and elongated feathery fin rays. They are fairly well known as their impressive looks and bold nature make them a beautiful and easy subject for underwater photographers.

They have numerous other common names, such as lionfish, turkeyfish, firefish, peacock cods, zebra cods and tiger cods; some names refer to their appearance and others to their very painful sting.

The butterfly cods are reasonably distinct and share enough similarities to be recognisable to most people. Like stonefish, they are all members of the scorpionfish family and have 13 venomous spines along their backs. If threatened, they erect their spines toward the threat and may not retreat. Curious divers have been stung while trying to touch these fish. Like the related stonefish, they are mainly tropical in distribution and are usually associated with reefs and rocky outcrops.

Why Do Catfish Have Whiskers?

A catfish showing its venomous fin spines and prominent whiskers.

*T*he stout spines on the dorsal and pectoral fins of catfish can puncture human skin but the 'whiskers' are not part of their defence system. They are used to detect food and navigate through obstacles. 'Taste buds' are scattered all over the body and these are abundant in the whiskers so the direction of food can be located. At close range, this ability — combined with the catfish's well-developed sense of touch in its whiskers — can pinpoint food even when it is buried in mud and silt. A blind catfish could still find food — and indeed many species have very small eyes — but a catfish that loses its whiskers would probably be in serious danger of starving to death.

How Did the Pufferfish Get Its Name?

*A*lthough pufferfish have poisonous flesh and a bad taste, they are not fast swimmers and are still at risk from predators unfamiliar with them. To avoid being swallowed by a predator, some of these fish inflate themselves as an additional defence. They do this by gulping down water — or if removed from the water, they swallow air instead — until the body cavity is swollen like a balloon — sometimes to such an extent that the fish's vent protrudes.

This mechanism can work in one of two ways. It can make a pufferfish appear too large to swallow so predators seek a smaller meal instead. If a pufferfish is already in the mouth of the predator the effect is rather more personal. The puffer's sudden inflation, combined with the taste of its poisonous flesh and sometimes accompanied by prickly puffer-fish skin, generally causes the predator to spit it out and to be more careful about what goes into its mouth in future. When the danger has passed, the pufferfish releases the swallowed water or air and swims quietly away.

By inflating itself, a pufferfish can surprise its predators.

What Is Ciguatera Poisoning ?

*T*his is a sort of food poisoning which occurs after eating certain reef fish at certain times or locations. What happens is that tiny single-celled animals, called dinoflagellates, are eaten by small reef fish that graze the seaweeds on which they live. The dinoflagellates contain a poison called ciguatoxin which does not affect the fish but does accumulate within their tissues, becoming more concentrated with every meal.

Many reef fish, including this Lyretail Trout, can cause ciguatera poisoning in humans.

Eventually larger fish eat these smaller fish — also without being affected by the poison — and the poison becomes further concentrated. Still bigger fish, such as Jacks, Coral Trout, eels and Barracuda, then eat these fish and the poison once again concentrates in their tissues. The next link in the chain can then be people who, unfortunately, react very badly to ciguatoxin and may become violently ill having eaten an infected fish.

How Can I Avoid Ciguatera Poisoning ?

*C*iguatoxin is odourless, tasteless and colourless so it is very hard to detect in a fish. If you are eating out and fancy reef fish for your dinner, choose a reputable fish restaurant. Never eat fish from an area known to be infected with the dinoflagellates, especially at the same time of year as the last outbreak.

If you are catching reef fish to eat, do not take predatory ones over the 10 kg mark; the bigger the fish, the more concentrated the poison is likely to be.

Cooking the flesh of fish infected with ciguatoxin will not destroy the poison. To take what precautions you can, wash the body cavity of the fish thoroughly and discard all guts, gonads and gills, and remove the head.

If you are fishing in the tropics for big fish, ciguatera poisoning is always an issue.

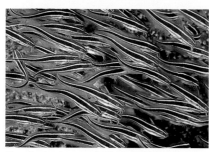

Even the tiny, innocuous-looking striped catfish can sting.

Catfish

Many species of catfish are found around Australia's coast and in some inland rivers. They can vary in size and shape depending on species, with some growing to no more than 10 cm and others reaching up to 2 m long. The tail fin may be forked like a salmon or have a fin along its length like an eel — hence salmon-tailed and eel-tailed catfish. All have obvious fleshy 'whiskers' around their mouths, which they use to detect food.

Although many catfish are good to eat, take care because they all have venomous fin spines, like scorpionfish. The dorsal and pectoral fins behind the head each have one stout spine and associated venom gland. If these spines puncture the skin, extremely unpleasant pain and swelling results. Wear stout gloves when handling catfish; even these will not provide complete protection as the spines are very sharp. If you intend to keep the catfish for food, kill it and carefully remove the head and the three fin spines — dead catfish can still sting.

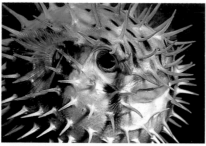

Porcupine fish have poisonous flesh and should not be eaten.

Toadfish and Pufferfish

Toadfish, pufferfish and their allies — the porcupinefish, boxfish and the giant Sunfish or Mola Mola — are all well known for their poisonous flesh. If eaten, humans can die. In Japan, the flesh of some species, called fugu, is specially selected and prepared by experts for eating. Fugu restaurants are carefully monitored and have special licences to prepare these dangerous fish. Even so, death by fugu poisoning is an annual event.

Many species in this deadly family live in the sea around Australia. They are frequently caught on hooks and lines. Handling them is safe as the poison is not absorbed by contact but always wash your hands afterwards and especially before handling food or wiping your mouth or eyes. Large species caught by anglers should be unhooked with care as many have powerful parrot-like jaws quite capable of removing a finger. Take care, too, when wading or diving where large species are about — there have been several instances of amputated fingers and toes.

TIGHT SECURITY

The entire head and body of a boxfish is encased in a hard box-like armour. Certain species even have protective spines on their bodies. Those with a pair of horns projecting from their heads are commonly known as 'cowfish'... for obvious reasons.

A non-banded form of the Chinaman Fish, a poisonous species.

Chinaman Fish

The Chinaman Fish is a type of 'snapper'. Adults measure 38–80 cm in length. They are found off the north coast of Australia in tropical rock and coral reefs. A Chinaman Fish can be recognised by its reddish or pink belly and usually banded appearance (although sometimes they are not banded). It also has a furrow in front of its eye.

This is a fairly common fish in some areas and, due to its large size, many anglers would be quite tempted to eat it. Indeed it is quite commonly eaten in parts of the Indo-Pacific and was eaten in Australia before it was discovered that this species can cause ciguatera poisoning. Do not eat it and warn any anglers you see catching Chinaman Fish of the dangers involved in doing so.

WARNING

Three ciguatera-carrying species of reef fish have been banned from sale in Queensland. They are the Chinaman Fish, the Red Bass and the Paddletail. Unfortunately the number of potential carriers of ciguatera poison is much greater than these three and currently numbers around 400 species.

Paddle Tail

This fish is found in similar localities and habitats to the Chinaman Fish and is also likely to carry ciguatera poison at times. It can grow to around 60 cm and the broadly forked paddle-like tail, large eyes and protruding mouth should help to distinguish it from other species. If there is any doubt, do not risk eating it. Always check with local fishing authorities before eating something you are unfamiliar with or from an area where ciguatera has been recorded.

Do not eat Paddle Tails: they can cause ciguatera poisoning.

The third Australian-known carrier of ciguatera poisoning is the Red Bass or Bohar Snapper. About 90 cm long and with a furrow in front of its eyes like the Chinaman Fish, it usually has a dark brown back with red or pink horizontally striped sides. The tips of the pectoral fins are long and dark. It is sometimes confused with the safe-to-eat Mangrove Jack. If in doubt, throw it back.

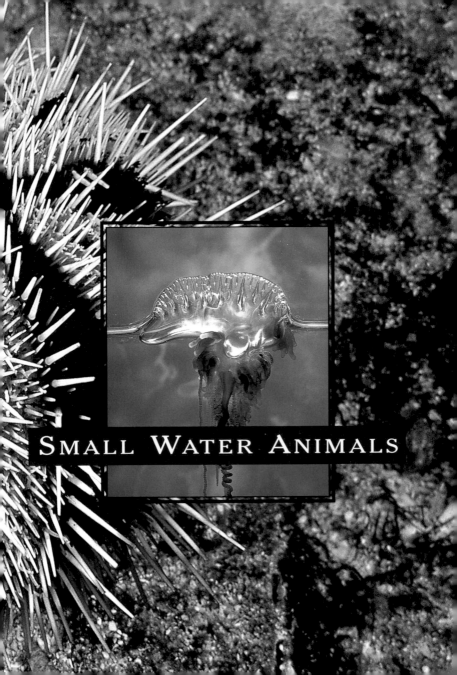

SMALL WATER ANIMALS

Can Fresh Water Harbour Hidden Dangers?

*T*he size of an animal is no indication of the potential problems it can cause — once-drinkable mountain streams can harbour diseases caused by minute parasites. Indeed some of the most dangerous diseases to humans are carried by small animals that depend, at one stage or another in their life cycle, on fresh water. Perhaps most notable is the mosquito. These creatures are capable of transmitting a variety of nasty diseases (see pages 45, 47 and 50). Although airborne as an adult, mozzie larvae live in fresh water, including shallow pools and tiny soaks.

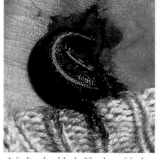

A feeding land leech, like those of fresh water, can cause quite profuse bleeding but it will drop off eventually.

Another group of moisture-loving creepy crawlies are the leeches (see page 51). Although these blood-suckers are extremely unpleasant when they latch onto your skin, they are unlikely to cause long-term damage. Once sated, they drop off, leaving little more than an itchy wound that will heal within days.

One small freshwater fish that is considered harmful in Australia is the Bullrout. Most people only find out about this little freshwater scorpionfish when they step on one and feel the pain. To avoid the spines piercing your flesh, wear plastic shoes when wading through freshwater streams.

What Tiny Dangers Lurk in the Sea?

Split-thumb damage feels worse than it looks.

*T*he potentially problematic small water animals of the sea are more numerous and diverse than those found in fresh water. They occur in a variety of shapes and colours. Many are very attractive and they are often of unusual appearance, so well worth looking at. They range from active animals, such as split-thumbs (mantis shrimps), crabs, Fortesques and octopuses to relatively inactive, seemingly innocuous-looking things like corals, sea urchins, cone shells, jellyfish and starfish (sometimes known as sea stars). Appearances can be deceiving, however. Even some marine worms cause problems: harmful ones can resemble harmless species, so be cautious. As with most wild animals, look but don't touch, then there is little danger of being hurt.

Why Are Small Animals So Well Armed?

*F*or small animals, the world can be a very dangerous place. Many predators, both large and small, would readily try to eat any vulnerable small animal they might find, so protection is vital to their survival. Protection among small animals is achieved in many ways. To avoid becoming dinner for some larger creature, these animals often use camouflage, speed, spines, stings, painful bites, bad taste, poisonous flesh or venoms. The more potent the defence the better protected the animal is, so sometimes a combination of defences is used.

The humble bristle worm is surprisingly well armed.

ROCK AND ROLL

When investigating beneath rocks in rockpools, always roll the rock towards you, not away from you. This way any scary creatures that might harm you can escape away from you, not towards you. Always replace the rock just as you found it.

Building Up the Arms Race

Naturally, predators try to evolve a way around the defence, so an escalating 'arms race' ensues, with defence and counter-defence developing between predator and prey. For example, many animals try to eat jellyfish so the venom in the jellyfish's stinging tentacles, which is used for catching prey, can also be used for defence. Some predators develop immunity to these mild stings, so natural selection favours those jellyfish with more potent venom. Some predators then develop immunity to this more potent venom and so it goes on. The end result is some exceedingly well-protected small animals — so beware.

Are You Sure It's Empty?

*W*hen exploring the seashore, don't pick up empty bottles or cans without checking for small inhabitants, such as a blue-ringed octopus. If you want to examine specimens closely, make sure you can accurately identify any animal you intend to handle. If you are not sure what an animal is, don't touch it — just in case. If you are going to an isolated area, include someone in your group who knows basic first aid associated with water animals.

Beware dipping hands or feet in rock pools...you may find more than you bargained for.

Blue-ringed Octopuses

A Greater or Northern Blue-ringed Octopus shows its rings as a warning. Inset: A blue-ringed octopus, not flashing its rings.

Several species of blue-ringed octopus are found around Australian coasts and in Indo-Pacific waters. With bodies the size of golf balls or less and armspans of about 15 cm or less, all are characterised by their small size. Like most octopuses, their body colours can change according to backgrounds but, when disturbed, all these octopuses display iridescent blue rings, spots or lines.

Blue-ringed octopuses take up residence in small cavities, such as shells, rock cavities or even submerged bottles and cans. While males tend to roam, dedicated mothers guard their eggs with great attention until they are hatched. The octopuses mainly eat crustaceans, chiefly crabs, which are quickly despatched with a venomous bite. Like all octopuses, their lives are short. Soon after breeding, both males and females die.

Self-Inflicted Bites?

Thanks to the publicity these notorious octopuses are well known and bites are extremely rare these days. Tourists and small children are perhaps most at risk but both these groups are usually well informed. In almost every case of a human being bitten the octopus was removed from the water and placed on bare skin. Victims were often showing off the attractive animal to friends. The bite is virtually painless and frequently goes unnoticed although the venom is a powerful neurotoxin (effects the nerves) and deaths have been recorded within 90 minutes. Paralysis begins to set in, often starting with speech difficulties, numbness, poor coordination and blurred vision. Respiratory difficulties or failure follows. Keep them breathing, even if this must be maintained for several hours, and recovery chances are very good.

Cone Shells

Cone shells can cause fatalities if they are handled. Inset: A close-up of the venomous barbed darts of a cone shell.

Cone shells are 1-12 cm long molluscs. They are related to garden snails but live in the sea, where they are widespread. Many are potentially dangerous to humans — particularly those occurring in the coastal waters of northern Australia. The cones are commonly found around coral reefs and rocky outcrops — occasionally crossing from one reef to another on bare sand. All cone shells are predatory and 'harpoon' their prey and predators with a venomous barbed dart. The dart is ejected from a highly mobile proboscis that extends from the front of the shell. Worms, molluscs and small fish are common targets. The expandable mouth cavity of many species is so capacious that even large prey can be swallowed whole.

Cone shells considered most dangerous to humans are usually fish-eaters. Their highly mobile and extendable proboscis can reach your fingers however you picked them up. Because species are difficult to identify, all cone shells should be treated with caution.

Beauty Leads to Demise

Cone shells are in far more danger from us than we are from them. Sadly their brightly coloured ornate shells are popular with collectors and consequently many species are becoming quite scarce. In some areas, one of their main predators is the Loggerhead Turtle, which can devour an entire meal of cone shells without ill effect — shells and all.

> **ABOUT-FACE**
> While it is most common for vertebrates, such as fish, to eat invertebrates, in the case of the slow-moving cone shells, the situation is reversed: cone shells eat the fish. Often these fish are almost as large as the cone shells themselves.

Soft but Smart?

*O*ctopuses are extremely intelligent animals. Several octopuses have been trained to remove corks from bottles or even remove lids from screw-topped jars for the food reward inside. Octopuses have very quick reflexes. They have large eyes that are similar to our own and eight very mobile arms. These dexterous arms are capable of fine manipulation and are used to locate and extract tiny struggling prey from beneath rocks, as well to build small lairs out of rocks and shells. They also use them to stroke one another gently when courting. Octopuses must learn to exploit new food sources and homesites quickly as there is a lot of competition. Their good vision and well-developed sense of touch requires a large brain to co-ordinate activity and interpret all the information. In fact, the brain of an octopus is roughly the size of one of its eyeballs. Interestingly octopuses have very short life spans and usually only live a year or less. All that learning and so little time to use it.

Octopuses are brainier than you think.

How Does an Octopus Change Colour?

*O*ctopuses change colour by opening and closing small spots of pigment in their skin called chromatophores in response to light, emotion, reproductive state or background colours. There can be up to 200 chromatophores per square millimetre of skin. Many octopuses also possess shiny reflective or refractive structures called iridocytes underlying some of these chromatophores. These may change or add a metallic sheen to the overlying colour. When some of the chromatophores are closed, the underlying iridocytes reflect back part of the spectrum as shiny iridescent blue.

Octopuses communicate with each other using colours and patterns. When courting, males flash at females who flash back different colours and patterns in response.

Most octopuses can change skin texture, too, to match their environment. An individual on the move may be smooth one minute and warty the next.

A close-up of the blue rings on a blue-ringed octopus.

What Kills Fast?

A cone shell's highly mobile proboscis, from which venomous barbs may be launched.

*C*one shells are particularly slow moving and of a small size, yet they feed on prey that is either faster than themselves or almost as large as themselves. This means their prey must be killed very quickly before it can get away or attack them — any prey that wanders too far after being stung is likely to be eaten by something else. A well-aimed barbed dart loaded with powerful, fast-acting venom expelled from a harpoon is the ideal weapon. The venom is a neurotoxin that may cause pain, swelling, loss of sensation at the sting site through paralysis, breathing failure, and sometimes death.

How Can I Stay Safe at the Beach?

*L*earn to identify dangerous molluscs such as cone shells and blue-ringed octopuses. The photos in this book are a good guide to the general appearance of some species. Never handle either of these animals with bare hands, even if you think it is dead or just an empty shell. Don't put shells that you are not sure about into your pockets. Digging around in coral or rocky rubble is not advisable; if you must, always wear thick gloves.

Children are attracted to brightly coloured things and may try to handle sea creatures that look pretty or interesting with unfortunate results. It is most important to supervise children in areas where blue-ringed octopuses or cone shells may be found. Unwary tourists are also at risk and should be warned of the dangers if you see them attempting to handle these animals.

OFFENSIVE BEHAVIOUR

Remember that most of the Great Barrier Reef is a national marine park and that means that it is an offence to take shells or coral from it, or to do damage of any sort to the living plants and animals that live there.

Beware seemingly empty shells: they may be occupied. Cone shells are very pretty but they can also be deadly.

Who Are the Echinoderms?

*T*he echinoderms are a strange group of invertebrates. Members include the sea urchins, the starfish, the brittle stars and the sea cucumbers. All these animals have radial symmetry, which means that they don't have a left and right side (or, in the case of sea cucumbers, a top and bottom) as all sides look much the same.

Starfish use a hydraulic system to move themselves around.

Hydraulics rather than muscles power their tube feet, spines and pincer-like pedicellariae. They usually have calcareous 'exoskeletons' or spicules of calcium in their skins. Their simple digestive systems allow some starfish to pass their stomachs out of their mouths to digest their food in situ and some sea cucumbers regurgitate their digestive tract as a defence, rather like a lizard dropping its tail.

Several species in each of these four groups of echinoderms are toxic in some way or an other, but most are harmless to humans.

Can You Eat Echinoderms?

The feeding tentacles of a sea cucumber. These animals are considered a great delicacy in some parts of the world.

*T*he gonads of sea urchins are regarded as a great delicacy in some countries and gonads are sometimes frozen for export. In some places sea urchins are now in danger of being overfished.

Another echinoderm, the sea cucumber, once formed the basis of a large industry in northern Australia. Collected at low tide around coral reefs, these animals were dried in the sun and sold as beche-de-mer or trepang to Asian markets. This market has now collapsed, however, due to overfishing.

What Are Pedicellariae?

Pedicellariae detail.

*T*he spikes of sea urchins usually look sharp enough to prevent most people touching them but sea urchins have several defences. In addition to their spines, which in some species are venomous, they often have lobed 'beaks' that project on stalks between the spines. These are called pedicellariae and they, too, can be venomous. Although rare, there has been at least one incident of a diver drowning as a result of envenomation by a flower urchin's pedicellariae.

This flower urchin is studded with pedicellariae.

How Do You Remove Spines?

SPIKES & BRISTLES

If in contact with echinoderms or bristle worms, wear gloves and/or protective clothing, such as a wet-suit. Some fish feed on bristle worms, so wear gloves when cleaning fish to avoid bristles in the gut. Take care, too, when rummaging through coral rubble, rocks or kelp as some sea urchins can puncture even protective clothing.

*S*ea urchin spines can be very difficult to remove. Wounds may bleed profusely, reducing visibility and making the spine slippery to grip. Spines are usually brittle and constantly break off. Sometimes, too, the urchin's skin around the spines dyes the flesh dark purple or brown making removal even harder. Treatment with hot water will often alleviate some pain but seek medical help as soon as possible to check that all the spine material is removed.

What Makes Bristle Worms Iridescent?

Brightly coloured bristle worms can sometimes bite or may cause rashes.

*T*he iridescent colours seen on some bristle worms are not actually there at all but are just an optical illusion, a trick of the light as in the blue rings of blue-ringed octopuses. The underlying colour of many iridescent rainbow hues is black but over this are layers of light-reflecting and light-refracting cells that split up the light and radiate it back as various colours of the spectrum. In bright light, the worm is quite colourful but in shade the same worm is comparatively dull. On the other hand, many bristle worm species are colourful in their own right, with bodies in shades of red and white, certainly testing the notion that worms are plain.

A flower urchin has venomous pedicellariae.

Sea Urchins

Sea urchins are found all around the Australian coast, usually in rocky, weedy or coral-reef situations — rarely over open sand. They graze on algae and seaweeds, some attaching themselves to kelp and detritus, possibly as protection or as an anchor against wave action. These complex little sea creatures, which may be 1–20 cm in diameter, have a suite of unusual structures which enable them to cling to surfaces, lodge in crevices, feed and move around.

Spines and tube feet are a common feature of echinoderms, the group to which sea urchins belong. They travel about by extending these tube feet beyond their spines to pull themselves along. Among the spines may be found the pedicellariae. These stalked three-jawed pincer-like structures, like the spines, can cause problems for unwary people (see page 85).

Sea urchins feed by grazing on tough seaweed, kelp and seagrasses. This they do by means of strong jaws called Aristotle's Lanterns. These structures are very efficient and some sea urchin species have been blamed for clearing large areas of aquatic vegetables, leaving the area unsuitable for baby fish.

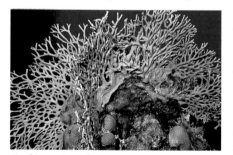

Brushing against a fire coral can cause a nasty sting.

Fire Coral

Fire corals are found mainly in tropical coastal areas, although some species live farther south, usually in shallow water. Often branched a bit like staghorn corals but softer, these corals can also take the form of flat, inter-connected structures, palm-like foliage or simple encrustations like sponges.

Fire corals vary in colour according to species but they usually do not have the bright pigments of many of the hard true corals. They are generally found in bays and on rocky or coral reefs. Like the true corals, to which they are related, they capture small organisms from the plankton, stinging them with stinging cells called nematocysts. Swimmers and divers brushing against fire coral may also be stung and suffer anything from mild itching to quite severe stings with associated red weals. Because of this, these animals have been given such common names as fire corals, stinging corals and itching corals.

Crown of Thorns Starfish: venomous spines.

Crown of Thorns Starfish

The tropical Crown of Thorns Starfish is usually found on coral reefs, its main food being coral polyps. Reaching 70 cm in diameter, it is covered in spines on its top. These sharp, brittle spines are covered with three layers of skin plus associated venom glands. If an unwary swimmer brushes against them, the spines can easily penetrate the skin and break off. Embedded spines cause excruciating pain and inflammation. The wounds are slow to heal, especially if material remains inside. After a painful encounter, divers are also at risk of drowning or of surfacing too quickly, which can result in 'the bends'. This dangerous condition arises from nitrogen that has been absorbed into the bloodstream under pressure during a deep dive. On a quick ascent the nitrogen forms bubbles in the blood. An affected diver may then arch their back or stand strangely — hence 'the bends'.

Bristle Worms

Bristle worms can cause bites or rashes.

Related to earthworms, marine bristle worms may be 5 cm – 1 m long. They typically have rows or tufts of pale or iridescent bristles along their bodies. Species with a compact shape may be known as 'sea mice'. Potentially troublesome species are found all around the coast but more often in the tropics. They live beneath coral and rocky rubble; some burrow into sand. Their diet includes small animals, carrion and algae.

Some bristle worms inflict painful bites that are mildly venomous. Of more lasting effect are the bristles of calcium carbonate or chitin that break off in the skin of people who inadvertently brush against the worms. The effects, which can last for several days, vary from itching to a painful blistered rash. With their iridescent skin or brightly coloured bristles, some species look quite attractive and children should be warned not to pick them up.

POPULAR BAIT

The Giant Beach Worm used for bait is a bristle worm that can give a nasty nip. Endangered in places due to over-harvesting, many wish it could be farmed but this is impractical as it has a larval stage that is spent out at sea.

How Do Jellyfish Sting?

*J*ellyfish belong to a group known as cnidarians. These include the sea anemones, corals and hydrozoans. All cnidarians possess nematocysts, which are capsules containing a coiled stinging thread, associated venom gland and a trigger 'hair' (or hairs). When something brushes against the trigger, either a chemical or mechanical action causes the coiled thread, which is loaded with barbs, to shoot into the victim, often embedding itself in its tissues. The coiled hollow thread of the nematocyst keeps the prey from escaping and venom and tissue-dissolving fluids are pumped into the victim via this hollow thread to both kill it and start the digestion process. The nematocysts will continue to sting and pump venom even if torn free of the cnidarian's body.

The dark dots inside these tentacles are nematocysts.

Do Animals That Eat Jellyfish Get Stung?

*M*any animals, from fish and turtles down to marine slugs and snails, feed on jellyfish with impunity. Some fish produce thick layers of protective mucus, which is either too great for the nematocyst to penetrate or does not stimulate its trigger. Others, such as turtles, have skin that is too hard and thick to be penetrated. Purple-raft Snails, which often share the fate of being blown onto beaches with bluebottles, can also swallow the nematocysts of bluebottles whole without being stung.

Remarkably, some nudibranchs, such as the lizard-shaped sea slug known as a sea lizard, eat nematocysts, pass them through their gut wall and into their own protective appendages for use in their own defence. So it is quite possible to be stung by a sea lizard's 'second-hand' stinging cells.

Tentacle-feasting sea lizards.

MYSTERY STINGERS

Sea-nettles and sea-lice are often named as the culprits for itching or stinging sensations in the sea but many of these 'encounters' are in fact with invisible broken-up, but still stinging, pieces of jelly-fish tentacle. Other so-called 'sea-lice' are in fact the larvae of parasitic worms, which normally burrow into the flesh of sea birds to complete their life cycle (for example, 'pelican itch'). If they bore into humans by mistake they die but their dead bodies still itch.

When Do Jellyfish Sting?

Beach stinger warning signs: heed them!

*S*eptember to March is the main season for jellyfish stings in the tropics, so avoid swimming at beaches during these times. At other times make sure someone is always close by in case you get into difficulties. Some beach life-saving clubs advertise that they have first-aid knowledge and supplies of Box Jellyfish antivenom, so seek out those beaches to swim at. Certain other beaches are netted against the larger jellyfish species, so you can swim in the netted areas. Use your common sense: supervise children and do not jump in where you are not sure what is in the water. Finally, believe the 'beach stinger' warning signs. In the past, waders and divers wore pantyhose over exposed flesh as the nylon did not trigger the stinging response. Although this is quite effective, all exposed areas of skin must be covered. Nowadays most divers prefer to wear special diving suits that cover all exposed areas thereby ensuring their complete safety.

Which Way Does the Wind Blow?

*B*luebottles are at the mercy of the winds. An onshore current can blow vast numbers directly onto a beach where they will perish. To compensate for this there are 'right-handed' and 'left-handed' bluebottles, this being based on the orientation of the float. If the prevailing wind blows the 'right-handed' blue-bottles onto the shore then the 'left-handers' will be blown safely away and vice versa if the wind comes from another quarter.

The percentage of each in any given population is apparently fifty-fifty but the prevailing winds may strip most, if not all, of one type from the group. Next time you see bluebottles on the beach, look to see which way the float is curved — you can be sure that most of them have floats that curve in the same way while out at sea their luckier 'mirror image' siblings sail away safely.

Like the bluebottle, the Purple-raft Snail — despite its barnacle cargo — is at the mercy of the wind.

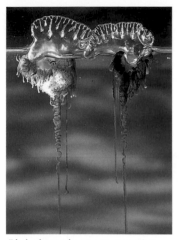

Bluebottle tentacles can cause nasty stings.

Bluebottles

Often called the man-o-war, bluebottles are notorious for their stings. This jellyfish is actually a colony of animals — the float is one individual; the feeding, stinging and reproductive tentacles are others. Each has a job to do and without it the colony fails. Bluebottles are widely distributed around the coast but are more commonly seen in summer, at least in southern regions, when onshore winds blow them onto the beaches. The float can be angled to catch the wind but colonies are really at its mercy. Those blown onshore dry up and die.

Bluebottles feed on plankton and small fish, which they sting to death with their long tentacles. Although the float is only up to 7 cm across, the tentacles can reach several metres. Broken pieces of tentacle can still sting, even without the rest of the jellyfish. The stinging cells, known as nematocysts, fire a barbed structure loaded with venom into their prey. The venom is then pumped into the victim on contact.

The Box Jellyfish is extremely dangerous to humans and has caused several fatalities.

Box Jellyfish

The world's most dangerous jellyfish, the Box Jellyfish, is found around the tropical coast of Australia. It is most common in the warmer months, particularly around the mouths of estuaries and mangrove areas, where breeding seems to occur. As its name suggests, it has four corners, each with a mass of trailing stinging tentacles designed to catch its prey of small fish and other animal plankton. Humans that come into contact with these tentacles, even in very shallow water, are stung in the same way.

This jellyfish is an active swimmer and can be quite large, up to 30 cm across, with the tentacles stretching more than 2 m. Several animals consume Box Jellyfish without any ill effects, including several species of endangered sea turtles.

A sting from the Irukandji could be deadly.

Irukandji

This jellyfish is mainly a tropical species but jellyfish stings that produce similar symptoms have been recorded much farther south, including off Victoria. Possibly there is more than one species capable of giving this type of sting, or the Irukandji could have a much greater range than previously thought. Part of the mystery stems from the difficulty of finding these animals — they are tiny and transparent, about the size of a thumbnail. Each individual has four trailing tentacles that stretch to 90 cm or more.

The Irukandji is most often found in deeper water and is most likely to be encountered by divers, but numbers of them can be swept inshore by winds and currents. Stings are more usual in summer but little is known of this animal's life and habits. The intensity of the sting varies among victims — despite the jellyfish's size, some are life threatening.

Other Jellyfish

There are many other jellyfish around the Australian coast that can cause stings and, in some cases, perhaps even fatalities. Their appearances vary according to species; some are typically bell-shaped and others more square. Some are notorious enough to have acquired common names such as Purple People-eater, Jimbles or Sea Nettles. Like most jellyfish, these species are predatory. Their trailing tentacles will sting any small animals that blunder into them. The victims are then hauled up to the body of the jellyfish and consumed. Unfortunately contact with human skin causes the same stinging response.

The Purple People-eater is another stinger.

> **MYRIAD MINIS**
> Several species of tiny freshwater jellyfish under 25 mm sometimes occur in vast numbers in lakes and slow rivers. Harmless to humans, they drift about catching tiny aquatic animals such as water fleas.

How Can a Little Shrimp Hurt Me?

*M*antis shrimps are also called split-thumbs for a good reason: if picked up, most will not hesitate in piercing or delivering a razor-like cut to the restraining hand or fingers, often with remarkable speed and power.

There are two basic types of prey-dispatching 'claws'. 'Smashers' tend to feed on molluscs, crabs and other hard-bodied animals, smashing them open with powerful blows from club-like front limbs. Never underestimate their strength: a large one can smash through aquarium glass. A blackened thumbnail is considered a

The false eyes of this split-thumb are designed to make it look larger than it really is.

minor injury from handling one of these. 'Spearers', on the other hand, have serrated or pronged front limbs with which they impale their victims. Some also have sharp tail spines to ward off blows by rivals, block entrances to their burrows or impale predators or unwary humans.

Mantis shrimps, or split-thumbs, live all around the Australian coast. Some species are as small as 1 cm; others grow to 40 cm. Often brightly coloured and intriguing looking, they may lurk in muddy or sandy burrows excavated in shallow seafloors, and in rock or coral shelters.

Who Are the Fortesques and Bullrouts?

*T*wo small scorpionfish that can deliver a potent sting are commonly encountered: the marine Fortesques and the freshwater Bullrouts. The small mottled Fortesques are only about 10 cm long. They usually inhabit estuaries, mangroves, rocky reefs and seagrass beds. Stings from their spines occur most frequently when well-camouflaged fish are stepped upon. Prawn collectors are often stung as they sort their catch — a good reason to wear stout gloves.

The saw-teeth spines of the small Fortesque.

Bullrouts grow to 30 cm and look rather like giant Fortesques. They are commonly found in fresh water. Well camouflaged, they lie in wait for passing crustaceans and small fish. If stepped upon, their sharp, venomous fin spines cause agonising pain and swelling. They can penetrate thin-soled shoes, which may need cutting off a swollen foot if they are not removed quickly. Even tiny Bullrouts inflict painful stings. Wear sturdy wading footwear in weedy, muddy or rocky coastal streams if you cannot see the bottom.

Are Any Crabs Dangerous?

*M*any species of reef crab are poisonous to eat and may cause symptoms similar to toad-fish poisoning. Species with black tips to their nippers should be regarded as suspect and avoided, particularly species of *Atergatis*, *Etisus*, *Zosimus* and *Lophozozymus*. Fatalities have been recorded overseas. Take any person feeling ill after eating a suspect crab to the nearest medical help, along with the crab shell.

Eating a Toxic Crab may result in itching, muscular paralysis and possibly death.

   Large crabs, such as mud crabs, are quite capable of painfully crushing a finger or hand with their powerful nippers. Breaking off the offending claw will not help as the crab is able to leave its clenched nipper attached to the victim while the rest of it makes good its escape. Smash the joint of the claw with a rock or prise it apart with a screwdriver or other handy lever.

What Should Every Angler Know?

Some sponges can cause dermatitis.

*W*hen angling, remember that Fortescues and split-thumbs can also be caught with hook and line. If you hook one, take great care to unhook it safely. Never handle either split-thumbs or small scorpionfish with bare hands and wear sturdy thick-soled footwear if wading in muddy areas, seagrass beds or other places where these animals might be lurking. When prawning at night, take special care and use thick gloves — both Fortescues and split-thumbs are sometimes found among the catch. Make sure you take care when dealing with large crabs or freshwater crayfish. Many anglers prevent problems by binding the 'thumb' to the claw or the claw to the body but this involves manipulation and therefore some risk if you are inexperienced.

   Other things to be wary of include sea cucumbers as several species exude poisonous sticky thread-like matter that can cause serious problems if it gets in your eyes or mouth. Also avoid touching sponges as some species have been known to cause dermatitis on contact with the skin.

   The most effective way to avoid problems is to look but not to touch, unless you absolutely know what you are doing. It is important to instruct children about the potential dangers of fishing and always supervise them.

First Aid Checklist

When going to the assistance of others, always check first to see if the danger is still present — otherwise there may be two victims to rescue instead of one. A good, simple book on first aid should be carried whenever potentially dangerous situations might occur.

Type of Injury	Type of Animal	Type of First Aid
Envenomation	Venomous snakes Some spiders Scorpions Centipedes Ticks Ants Bees Wasps Platypus Jellyfish Cone shells Stonefish Scorpionfish Catfish Blue-ringed octopuses Some stingrays Fire coral Some sea urchins Some hairy caterpillars Some bristle worms	For very venomous animal bites, stings or cases where allergic reactions occur, a pressure immobilisation bandage may be required. Move the bitten limb as little as possible. Use a broad, preferably elasticised bandage and bandage over the bite then up and down the bitten limb about as firmly as for a sprained ankle but not so tight as to stop blood circulation. If foreign material is present (e.g. spines) see 'Bruising, punctures and lacerations'. Immobilise the limb using a splint. Keep the patient comfortable and reassure them. If semi-conscious, place them on their side. In some cases you may need to perform cardio-pulmonary resuscitation (CPR) and expired air resuscitation (EAR). Be sure to carry with you a basic first-aid book explaining these procedures when out in the field. Seek medical aid urgently. Immersing the affected limb under hot, but not boiling, water can help reduce pain from venomous fish or ray stings. Follow with a cold pack to reduce swelling. Try ice packs on lesser bites and stings e.g. Red-back Spider bites. Always seek medical assistance if the casualty is unsure or unwell.
Poisoning	Toadfish Some reef fish Cane Toad Some marine crabs	Seek medical assistance urgently. Reassure the casualty, if conscious. You may need to perform CPR and EAR (see above). Remember that toadfish poisoning can seem to leave the victim unconscious but in reality he or she is fully aware but paralysed — be careful what you say in their presence.

Type of Injury	Type of Animal	Type of First Aid
Bruising, punctures and lacerations	Australian Magpie Cassowary Emu Some kangaroos Feral pigs Crocodiles Dingo Brumbies Water Buffalo Some sharks Some stingrays Some eels Other fish bites Some sea urchins Split-thumbs Some bristle worms 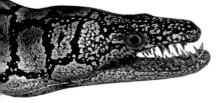	If there is no broken fish spine or other material visible, try to control blood loss by direct pressure over the wound. If foreign material is present, apply pressure around the wound. Elevation of the limb helps to slow blood loss. Severe blood loss may require a tourniquet but only as an emergency measure because irreparable damage can occur if the tourniquet is too tight or left on for too long. It is recommended to release tourniquets and re-apply (if necessary) every 20 minutes to minimise such damage. If wounds are minor, wash them under clean water to prevent further infection and apply bandages or sticking plaster to keep them clean. Cold compresses and ice packs reduce the swelling associated with bruises. Keep the patient warm and comfortable as shock may set in. Seek medical assistance. Spines and hairs of bristle worms and caterpillars can often be removed by applying and ripping off sticking plaster or adhesive tape. Protruding spines can be removed wherever possible, but medical help may be required for some cases.
Infection	Mosquitoes Ticks Mites (Septicaemia from Crocodiles, goannas or other animal bites)	Seek medical attention urgently if you feel ill after an insect, tick or mite bite. The best advice is to wear insect repellent when in areas where blood-sucking invertebrates live. Reddened and painful wounds that seem slow to heal can indicate secondary infections — seek medical advice.
Electrocution	Numbfish Torpedo rays	Where necessary, rescue casualty from water and perform CPR if required (see left-hand page). Most victims recover without the need for treatment.
Rashes	Some hairy caterpillars Some bristle worms	Make sure all spines, hairs and bristles are removed. Ice packs and calamine lotion may help in some cases. If rash or irritation persists, seek medical advice.

INDEX